COLLIERIE
SOUTH WAL

John Cornwell

Published by
Landmark Publishing Ltd,
Ashbourne Hall, Cokayne Ave, Ashbourne, Derbyshire DE6 1EJ England
Tel: (01335) 347349 Fax: (01335) 347303
e-mail: landmark@clara.net
web site: www.landmarkpublishing.co.uk

ISBN 1 84306 017 5

© **John Cornwell 2001**

British Library Cataloguing in Publication Data: a catalogue
record for this book is available from the British Library.

Print: Bookcraft, Midsomer Norton
Design: Mark Titterton

Front cover: The Pit heads at Wyndham with the Western shaft in the distance. Note the new or reconditioned chocks waiting to be taken underground.

Back cover: The last dram of coal raised at Tymawr Colliery in June 1983.

COLLIERIES OF SOUTH WALES:1

A collier from Coegnant Colliery

John Cornwell

Landmark Publishing

CONTENTS

INTRODUCTION

Ten years have now elapsed since the closure of Deep Navigation Colliery, the last of the major colliery closures. I feel that now is the time to put on record some of the more interesting and historical collieries and their workforce, before they are nothing more than a distant memory.

In 1975 there were 47 working collieries and a number of colliery sites still maintained as pumping and ventilating units, like Tirpentwys, Clydach Merthyr, and many others. In the course of my work underground as a photographer to record the modern side of the industry, I was also allowed access on the surface and underground to record the historic buildings, machinery and underground workings of the South Wales Coalfield.

In the process of recording the industry I developed a technique of using the camera on a tripod with an open lens and using either a standard cap lamp or approved Locomotive lamp which had two batteries as opposed to one on a cap lamp. The lighting had to be approved as almost all photographs were taken in an atmosphere which normally contained firedamp, and flash was strictly forbidden. With this technique I developed a system of photographing shafts 1000 ft deep, long lengths of roadways or portraits of men and objects sometimes only 3 ft from the camera.

I apologise if a particular colliery has been omitted, as there is a limit to what can be put into one book. It may be possible one day to produce a further book covering other collieries and early pre-National Coal Board sites. South Wales still has many interesting historical sites, despite the massive programme of clearance, some of which was not really necessary.

The object of this book is to place on record some of the history of the technology of the South Wales Coalfield with its workforce. The book is not a definitive history, it is only a brief look into what was a large and very important industry which has almost disappeared.

I have refrained from commenting on the closure of the Coalfield, as others may well voice their feelings better than I could.

John Cornwell
Hallatrow
North East Somerset

Abernant Colliery was situated in a wide open valley which is bounded by the Gardener's Fault to the east and the Duffryn Fault to the west: the valley is also crossed by east-west thrust planes. As at Cynheidre the geological structure proved much more complex than originally anticipated.

The sinking of Abernant Colliery was commenced in 1954 and completed in 1958 at a cost of £10 million, to work the Red Vein at a depth of around 1,200ft. The shafts were also sunk down to a point just below the Peacock Vein which is said to be the finest anthracite in the world, at a depth of No. 1 shaft 2,510ft and the No. 2 2,961ft. In the early days of working the colliery encountered severe geological conditions, which were overcome. By the late 1970s the colliery take was eight square miles with 44 miles of underground roadways, with more than 10 miles of high-speed belt conveyors. The colliery was one of the first mines to work on the retreat system of mining.

Closure came in 1988.

Above: General View taken in 1980.

Opposite page: Pumping station at pit bottom in 1978.

Above: Heading at Abernant with a Dosco-in-seam-miner, 1978.

Opposite page: A typical road at Abernant Colliery with mine car on cable haulage. Note the Becorit mono rail.

The business end of the Dosco machine, 1978.

AMMANFORD COLLIERY
AMMANFORD, CARMARTHEN

The colliery was sunk as two slants in 1891 by the Ammanford Colliery Company to work the Little Vein which was 3ft high; later the Big Vein was worked.

Only the No.2 slant worked into the period of the NCB and this mine ceased work in 1976. When the New Bettws Mine was ready to commence production, most of the men transferred to it.

This mine was, with Graig Merthyr Colliery, the last in the South Wales Coalfield to raise coal to the surface in journeys of trams. The colliery was also one of the last to work by hand a longwall timbered face, certainly the last in the anthracite area.

Colliery Sign

Above: Journey of empty trams being lowered into the slant in 1974.

Left: The slant entrance in 1974. With Graig Merthyr colliery this was the last colliery to use cable hauled journeys of trams.

Safety Officer inspecting the roof on the last face at Ammanford in 1974.

Above: Gerald Gibson drilling a shot hole on the face in 1974.

Right: Timbered longwall face in the Big Vein, 1974.

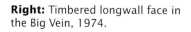

Preparing timber on the face in 1974.

Timber work on the last face in Ammanford slant, 1974.

BETWS MINE
GLAMORGAN

Betws was the last major mine to be sunk in the South Wales Coalfield and is now with Tower Colliery the only working mine left in South Wales.

Work on the Betws Mine was begun in 1974, a local firm Messrs. James Williams & Sons, Neath (1957) Limited, were the contractors. Two parallel tunnels were planned to be driven 150ft a week through hard rock for a distance of two and a half miles, dipping at gradients of 1 in 5 to 1 in 14. Soon after the start of the tunnelling tough water-bearing sandstone was encountered and the development soon fell behind by six weeks, but the Betws project was completed in the two and a half years allotted. The twin tunnels were driven in to the 5ft 3in. Red Vein, and retreat mining began in the early spring of 1978.

Men from the closed Ammanford Slant and Graig Merthyr mine comprised the workforce of 500. The mine was planned to produce 500,000 tons of coal a year from two coal faces with a third face held in reserve. In 1983 £12 million was allocated to the mine to extend the main access tunnels through the major geological disturbance known as the Gardener's Fault which formed the boundary of the workings of 1983 and in that year it was the industry's second most profitable pit.

A £3.9 million package was given in 1985 to sink a new wide shaft 1½ miles from the existing surface, the shaft being sunk to a depth of 620ft. At the same time a drift was driven underground to connect with the shaft. The 620ft shaft was cored in a continuous drilling programme which was planned to take 10 weeks. A huge rig was centred over the shaft opening and extracted the

Control room in 1976-77.

core by means of a rotating cutting head. Five miles away at Abernant the NCB spent £5 million to open out the additional reserves of anthracite which should have provided the mine with up to 15 years of additional production.

By 1986 Betws was producing about 12,000 tonnes of saleable coal per week at an output of 3½ tonnes per manshift; the mine employed 770 men of which 680 worked below ground.

Betws Anthracite Ltd still continues in operation today producing high grade anthracite.

Entrance to the newly completed mine with man riding cars and conveyor.

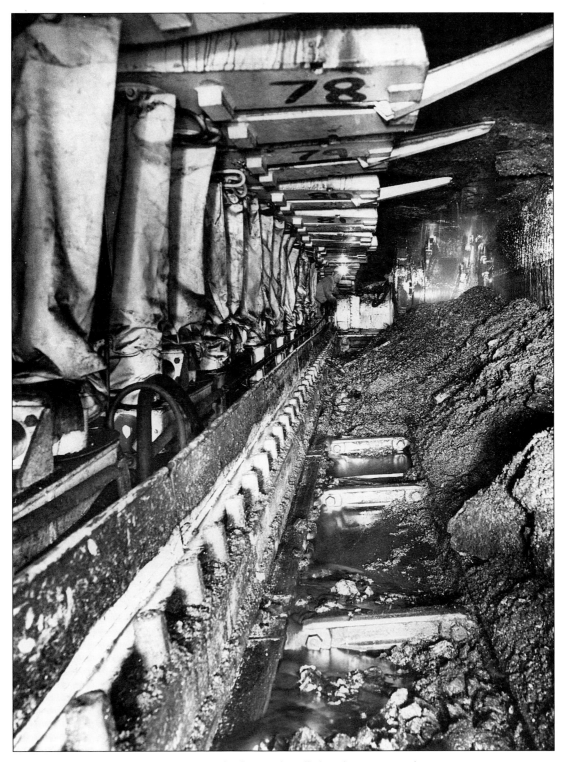

Chainless haulage on the face with Gullick Dobson powered supports.

The afternoon shift waiting for the manriding train.

Blaenavon Collieries
Blaenavon, Monmouth

The first recorded working of coal in the Blaenavon area was in 1775, when William Tanner and Mary Gunter were granted a lease to work coal. The early workings were patch works and small levels situated on and around the extensive outcrop; many of these early sites still survive today to the north and west of Blaenavon.

It is probable that the first shaft to be sunk was the Engine Pit, which was sunk as a pumping pit. The sinking date is not known but would have been around 1800 to 1810; the Engine Pit Level would also have been driven about the same time.

The next major development would have been the sinking of the Cinder Pits, which are shown on the 1819 plan of Blaenavon, as intended Engine Pits for the deep work. The Cinder Pits were the scene of Blaenavon's worst mining disaster, on 28th November 1838 when torrential rain, after a heavy snowfall, ran off the hillsides and poured down the shafts of the Cinder Pits, drowning 14 men and two women.

Levels and collieries working before 1840:	
Aaron Brutes Level, c. 1800	Gain Pits, sunk around 1839
Black Pin Level, 1812	Gunter's Level
Bridge Level, 1782	Hill Pits, 1835
Cinder Pits, probable sinking 1819	Old Coal Pits
Dick Kear's Slope (New Slope), c. 1820	James Kearsley's Level
Engine Pit, 1800 to 1810	Old Slope
Engine Pit Level, 1800 to 1810	Parker's Level
Engine Coal Level, situated in the Iron Works yard	River Row Level
Forge Level, 1830?	Tunnel Level
Forge Pit	

After the erection of the New Furnaces at Forgeside by the Blaenavon Iron & Coal Co. in the 1840s, many new levels and pits were opened around the Forgeside Works:

Coity Pits, 1840	Forge Slope
Coity Level	Kearsley's Pit (later to be Big Pit)
Dodd's Slope, c. 1840	

Around 1878-79 Kearsley's Pit, which had been used as a ventilation shaft for the Forge Level and Pit, was deepened from the Threequarter seam depth of 128ft to the Old Coal at 293ft. The new colliery appeared in the Mines Inspectors' List of Mines as Big Pit in 1880, and by 1895 it was raising 5,000 tons of coal per week with Dodd's Slope.

Collieries Of The Blaenavon Iron & Steel Co. Ltd., 1900:

Colliery	Persons employed above ground	Persons employed below ground
Big Pit	370	200
Cinder Pits	Not worked since 1895	—
Dodd's Slope	179	26
Forge Slope	126	16
Gain Pits	149	17
Kay's Slope	328	54
Milfraen	199	23
Tunnel and Clay Level	35	6

Blaenavon Coal Seams:

Seam depth ft	Standard name	Local name	Thickness
76	Two Feet Nine	Elled	3ft 6in.
100	Upper Four Feet	Big Vein	3ft 0in.
127	Upper Six Feet	Threequarter	4ft 6in.
196	Upper Nine Feet	Horn or Top Rock	4ft 0in.
215	Nine Feet	Bottom Rock	5ft 6in.
224	Lower Nine Feet & Upper Bute	Black	
295	Yard	Meadow	3ft 6in.
311	Seven Feet	Yard	
370	Lower Five Feet & Gellideg	Old Coal	3ft 6in.
442	Garw	Garw & Engine Coal	2ft 6in.

BIG PIT, BLAENAVON, IN THE 1890s

Five of the seams were worked by the longwall system; the sixth, the Elled seam, was worked on the pillar and stall method, horses being employed in hauling from the face workings to the bottom of the main road. From this point the trams were hauled by steam engine to the pit bottom. There were four haulage engines in Big Pit supplied with steam from four Cornish boilers. One engine in the Old Coal had two 18in. cylinders, and worked a haulage plain over 3,600ft in length, with gradient of 1 in 12.

The original winding engine was constructed by Fowler Co. of Leeds. It had two 26in. horizontal cylinders and drums for flat ropes and could raise two trams in each cage.

Thirteen Cornish and egg-ended boilers supplied steam to the winding engine, and the engines on Dodd's and Forge Slopes. The upcast shaft for Big Pit was the Coity Pit which had a Waddle fan.

Opposite page top: The two entrances of Dick Kears Slope in 1975, the blocked entrance is to the left. The mine is shown on the 1883 O.S. map of the Blaenavon area.

Opposite page bottom: Big Pit Blaenavon in 1950 from the timber yard. At this time the pit was still wound by an 1880 Fowler Steam winder with flat rope.

Blaenavon Collieries, 1947-80			
Colliery		*Persons employed Below ground*	*Above ground*
1947	Big Pit	661	136
1958	Big Pit	908	151
1979	Big Pit	180	57
1980	Big Pit Closed	173	54
1947	Kay's Slope & Milfraen	281	69
1947	Garn Slope	541	137
1958	Garn Slope & Kay's Slope	547	126
1966	Garn Slope & Kay's Slope.	Closed	Closed

In 1973, coal winding at Big Pit ceased. A new drift had been driven near the washery enabling all coal to be raised, washed and blended on one site. From the late 1960s, all production was concentrated in the Garw seam. The maximum thickness of the Garw was 2ft 6in., its minimum 2ft 2in.

Until it closed in 1980, Blaenavon had some of the oldest workings in South Wales. Its drainage system was unique: it incorporated the Forge Level, Wood's Level and Kear's Slope, all of them dating back to 1830 and before, while the Engine Pit Level (c. 1810) was also retained as an emergency exit.

Today this complex comprises a UNESCO World Heritage Site; with a museum based upon the iron works and Big Pit, enabling the heritage of iron and coal mining in South Wales to be passed on to future generations.

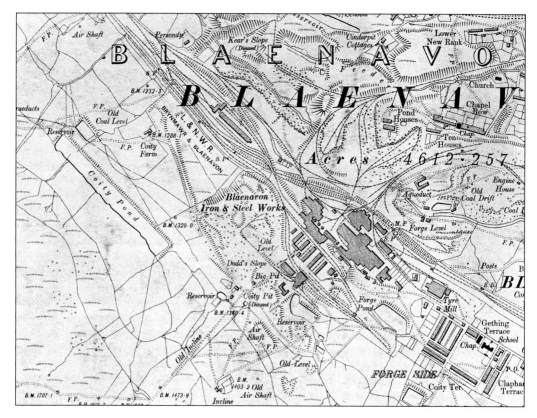

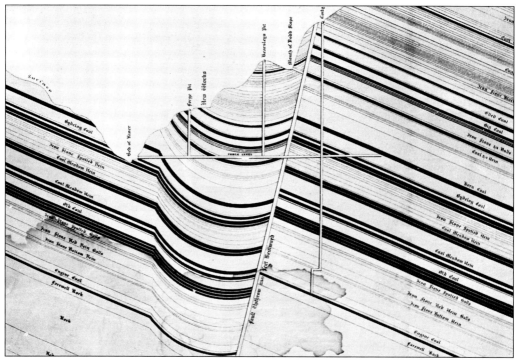

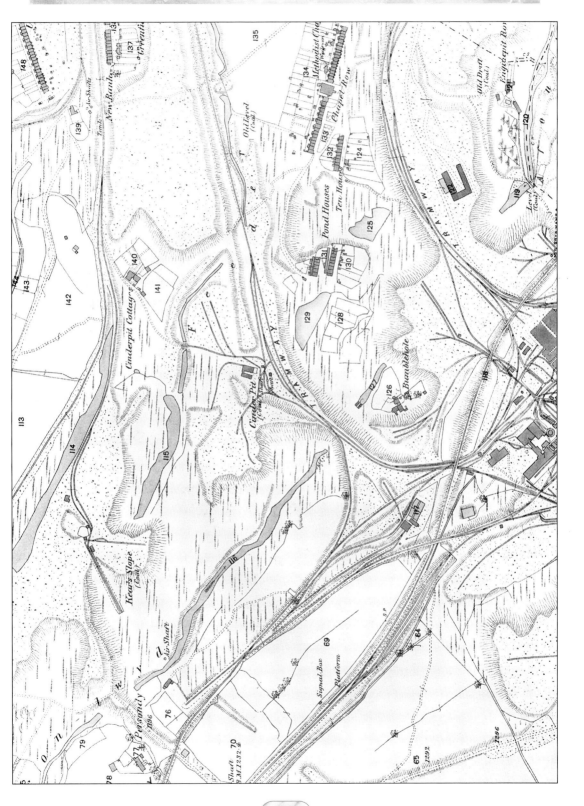

Above: General view of the Washery with the Garn Tips in background.

Below: The manager talking to a deputy in the yard, 1975.

The Engine Pit Level driven around 1810. This level was one of the oldest surviving mines in the Blaenavon complex and was kept as an emergency exit until 1979.

Above: A brick lined level in the Blaenavon complex, probably the Forge Level, taken in 1975.

Left: New roadway driven from the drift entrance with conveyor belt carrying coal from the Garw seam, 1978.

Above: The abandoned pit bottom in 1975.

Left: A plough on the G11 face, February 1979. This was the Garw seam, and was 28in. thick. It was the last seam to be worked in Big Pit.

Below: Bill Gunter, the Big Pit safety officer, on the G11 Face in 1979.

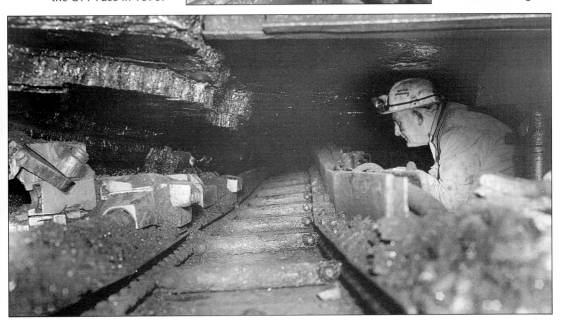

Above: A pit pony returning to Big Pit stable in 1968 after working
in one of the many levels in the complex.

Below: *Nora* an Andrew Barclay locomotive in 1973 working in the yard of the original Blaenavon
Iron Works. This line was used as the land sale yard.

Above: The tail gate on G11 face, the Garw seam, at this time the seam section was around 2ft 4in.

Above: The last day for Glyn Morgan, the final NCB manager, 28 November 1980.

Left: Bill Gunter standing at the archway to Dick Kear's Slope, driven around 1820.

Above: The Garn tips in winter.

Right: Engine Pit Level with decayed timbering, used as a emergency exit until 1979.

Opposite page: The River Arch Level driven some-time before 1840 and still in use today.

Above: The original entrance to Woods level now partially flooded. Since a waste tip in the vicinity of the entrance extended across the valley, the entrance was continually extended by adding steel rings. The River Arch level had to be extended in the same fashion.

Left: A mine official examining a section of a cage of a water balance machine, near the bottom of the Forge Pit 1975.

A fly wheel from a large steam haulage engine, used to support the pack wall
Engine Pit 1975-6.

BLAENGWRACH MINE
CWMGWRACH, NR. NEATH, GLAMORGAN

A mine was worked in this area by an Edward Protheroe as early as 1814. It may have opened out an ancient level, and in 1816 a tramroad was constructed from Blaengwrach to the Vale of Neath Canal. In 1903 the Empire Colliery was sunk into the earlier workings of Cwmgwrach level. In 1924 the original level was reopened as Cwmgwrach No.2 and in 1927 a further level was driven turning Cwmgwrach into a large concern employing almost 1,000 men.

After Nationalisation the NCB drove a new drift which was completed in 1962 and was known as Blaengwrach Mine which worked the Six Feet seam. The new mine's take was bounded by the Rhigos Fault to the east and the Glyncastle fault to the west with a down-throw of 1,200ft. The workings also contained the smaller Cwmgwrach Fault which divided the underground operations.

In the late 1970s the colliery drove into the Nine Feet seam, but unfortunately poor geology prevailed and the mine closed in 1983.

Close up of entrance taken in 1977.

Above: Modern concrete viaduct spanning the River and linking Blaengwrach Mine with the washery.

Left: General view of the new mine in 1977.

An almost perfect section of main road in Blaengwrach Mine, 1977.

Poor conditions near the face in 1977.

Hydraulic props and bars and a shearer in the Six Feet seam, 1977.

An Eimco machine in a development heading, possibly in the Nine Feet seam. Note the thick section of the seam.

This colliery was sunk and worked by Powell Duffryn prior to the outbreak of the World War I; the colliery passed to the NCB on Vesting Day in 1947.

The shafts Nos. 1 and 2 were sunk to a depth of 1,844 and 2,142ft, and all plant at the mine was driven by electricity. At the time of closure the original winding engines were still working.

The colliery was once described as a pit where nothing ever happened apart from raising coal, but it was very wet, and pumping had to raise between 7 and 9 million gallons of water every day.

By the late 1970s, 800 men raised an annual saleable output of 244,953 tons of coal from 2 faces in a take four miles square.

Closure came in 1983.

The two headframes which were typical of the Powell Duffryn Company.

The impressive original Siemens Electric winder was installed in 1910-14 and worked until closure in 1983.

The tub circuit at Britannia Colliery in 1977.

BRYNLLIW COLLIERY
GROVESEND AND
MORLAIS COLLIERY
LLANGENNECH, GLAMORGAN

Brynlliw was originally sunk in 1903 to 1908 by Thomas Williams (Llangennech) Ltd. to work the Swansea Four Feet seam, at a depth of about 1,020ft. By 1914 the Five Feet Seam was also developed but by 1927 the pit had closed.

The NCB reopened the pit in 1954 using the original shafts and headgear, investing £4.8 million, deepening the shafts, the driving of several thousand yards of new roadways for locomotive haulage. The No. 2 shaft was fitted with skip winding, and by 1968 the annual output was over 300, 000 tons from the Swansea Three Feet and Six Feet seams.

Morlais Colliery was also sunk by Thomas Williams in the 1890s on the site of an earlier slant, with a 13 ft diameter shaft which was partially unlined.

In 1976 a 957ft 9in. in roadway was driven from the Morlais workings passing under the estuary of the Afon Llwchwr to link up with Brynlliw Colliery to form a single unit which operated from 1977. This colliery was the last in the coalfield to use a steam winder on the shaft and steam haulage engine on the slant.

Both pits closed in 1983.

A view of Brynlliw Colliery before reconstruction in 1951.

General view of Morlais collery looking east across the River Afon Llwchwr, 1978.

The derelict pumping engine house which clearly contained a beam pump for which no information is now available.

The Andrew Barclay winding engine wound from the shallow 13 ft diameter shaft until closure in 1983.

Above: A heading with an Eimco machine in 1977.

Left: Brynlliw Colliery taken in 1978. The colliery offices baths and canteen are situated on the left of the picture.

A Peckett locomotive working in the yard in 1973.

Overmen inspecting a shearer on the Six Feet Seam in 1977; the chocks are by Gullick Dobson.

The colliery taken in 1978. The sidings and all railway track were removed and the coal was raised at Brynlliw Colliery until that pit also closed.

Above: The cave-like pit bottom in 1978, cut from the strong bed of sandstone, which needed no support.

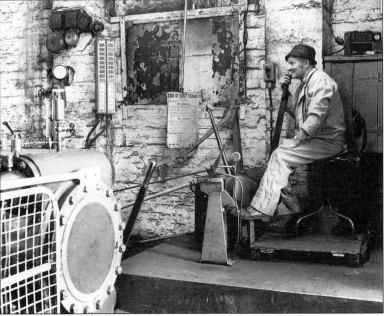

Left: One of the engine men on the Andrew Barclay steam winder, 1978.

Above: The Andrew Barclay Haulage engine which wound on the slant situated beside the pumping engine house.

Left: The two Lancashire boilers; the boiler on the right was the standby.

Sunk by the Newport Abercarn Black Vein Steam Coal Co., the colliery is first mentioned in the Inspectors' List of Mines in 1874. The original owners became a subsidiary of Partridge, Jones & John Paton between the two wars. There were three shafts, two for winding and one for ventilation only.

No. 1 Pit.	Downcast, elliptical 22ft by 18ft, depth 1059ft.
No. 2 Pit.	Upcast, 18 ft diameter, ventilation only, depth 900ft.
No. 3 Pit.	Downcast, elliptical 16ft by 12ft, depth 900ft.

Celynen South was one of the last collieries to raise coal with steam winding engines.

The colliery was working since the 1870s, the main seams being: Elled Big Vein, Threequarter Vein, Black Vein, Meadow Vein and Old Coal.

At Vesting Day nearly half the faces were hand cut and worked by the longwall heading and stall method; in 1983 all faces used powered supports with armoured conveyors and shearers.

Details of Steam Winding engines:	
No. 1 Pit.	Engine built by Robey of Lincoln, 24in. cylinders, 4ft stroke, engine taken out in 1970.
No. 2 Pit.	Converted steam haulage, built by Lewis of Treherbert.
No. 3 Pit.	Engine built by Fullerton, Hodgart & Barclay, removed in 1970.

Harvey of Hayle, Cornwall built a 85in. Cornish pump with a 10ft stroke in 1873 for the Newport Abercarn Black Vein Steam Coal Co. which was installed at Celynen Colliery at a cost of £3,500.

The pit closed on the 5 September 1985.

Celynen South c.1900, with two batteries of coke ovens; the NA stood for Newport and Abercarn.

Celynen South in 1978. This headframe by E. Finch and Co. of Chepstow, was built in the style of the old wooden headframes in 1877.

The miners 1984-85 strike at Celynen South Colliery.

The shaftsman at Celynen South in the shafts cabin, wearing a safety harness.

Props and bars and a chain of the haulage system 1977.

Trams and creeper at the pit bottom, 1977.

The blacksmiths' shop, with six forges.

Demolition at Celynen South in 1985.

The Neath Colliery Company commenced sinking a pair of shafts in 1921 on the east bank of the Dulais River, but the sinking was suspended until 1924. In 1928 the Amalgamated Anthracite Collieries acquired Cefn Coed Colliery and completed the work. The Big Vein was found at a depth of 2,250ft, and the Peacock Seam was reached in 1931. The three main seams worked were: The Dulais, Peacock, Nine Feet and White Four Feet.

Engine house for the Markham engine on the upcast shaft, 1973.

The Colliery closed in 1968 when a new drift mine to be known as Blaenant Mine was opened, which still retained the use of the two steam winders on the old Cefn Coed shafts. A Worsley Mesnes steam winding engine was situated on the downcast shaft with a Markham Steam Winder on the upcast shaft; these engines were said to have been installed around 1927. The Worsley Mesnes winder still stands on the downcast shafts in its engine house alongside the impressive battery of Lancashire boilers and is now the centrepiece of the Cefn Coed steam museum .

After the closure of Cefn Coed Colliery a short-lived drift operated for a few years until the New Blaenant Drift was commissioned to work the No.2 Rhondda Seam. A 1,984ft conveyor plane at a gradient of 1 in 3.7 was driven. A modern manriding train carried 120 men into the mine, passing over the River Dulais in a covered bridge which carried the outgoing conveyor. The mine had 10 miles of underground roadways, with three miles of high-speed conveyors.

Despite the rich fault-free deposits the mine was closed on 11 May 1990, having worked from the late 1970s.

Right: Engine house and headframe on the downcast shaft in 1973. The winder, a Worsley Mesnes, is now preserved with the boilers and is now known as the Cefn Coed Steam Centre.

Opposite page: Lancashire boilers for the two steam winders at Cefn Coed Colliery, 1973.

The Markham steam winder of 1927, now broken up.

The Worsley Mesnes winder of 1927 in 1973. It is now preserved.

Maintenance men on a new face just installed. Taken in the early 1980s.

The afternoon shift waiting on the manriding train, Blaenant Colliery in the late 1970s.

Above: A 42in. conveyor in the main roadway at the bottom of the new drift. This conveyor could clear coal from the two double-shifted faces in the No.2 Rhondda seam at a rate of 600 tons an hour. The track on the left is for the manriding train and supplies.

Left: Rackatrack chainless haulage with Gullick chocks on a new face at Blaenant Colliery in the late 1970s.

This interesting colliery was situated in the Lower Clydach Valley about 7 miles to the north of Swansea. The Colliery which was a drift or slant was opened around 1863 by the Clydach Merthyr Company Ltd. to work the Graigola seam which had been worked in the area since the 1820s.

The slant was mainly 12ft wide and 7ft high and struck the Graigola seam at a distance of 1,050 ft from the entrance. The mine was extremely interesting as it contained an underground blacksmith's forge installed in the Graigola seam and underground boilers, which were thought to be working until the late 1940s. A return airway terminated in a stack situated close to the entrance in the side of the valley, and there was a Waddle fan 20ft in diameter made in 1880 driven by an engine with a 18in. cylinder and a 30in. stroke.

This mine closed in 1961, but was retained as a pumping station for Graig Merthyr Colliery which ceased working in 1978. The mine was later dismantled and sealed.

The underground blacksmith's shop situated in the Graigola seam.
It is thought that the forge worked until the late 1940s.

Above: The Waddle fan and the engine house which contained a high speed steam engine. The stack in the background was connected by a drift to the boilers which also provided additional ventilation.

Opposite page: The drift from the boilers which led outbye to the stack.

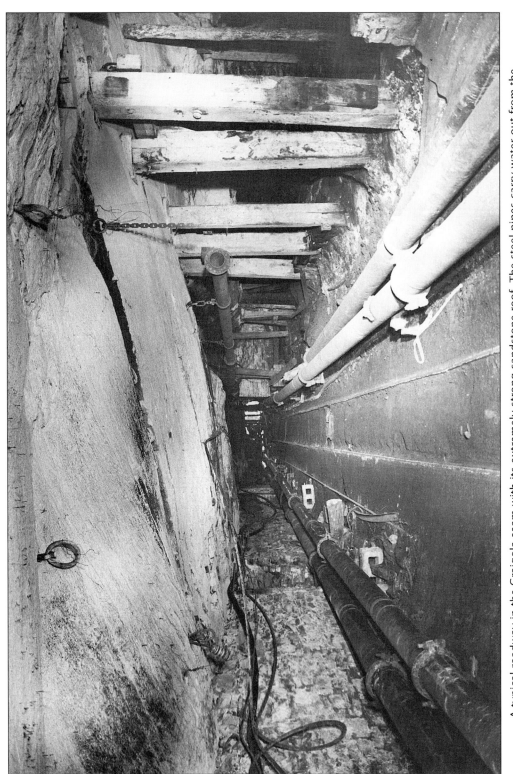

A typical roadway in the Graigola seam with its extremely strong sandstone roof. The steel pipes carry water out from the pumps to discharge into the valley.

The colliery was certainly worked by North's Navigation Collieries Ltd in 1891, but it is possible that the original sinking may have been carried out by the Llynfi and Tondu Iron Co. in the 1880s. By the 1890s the colliery was raising around 1000 tons per day. The pit had two shafts, the North Pit and the South Pit which commenced winding coal in 1890. The coal was raised on the North Pit by a high pressure horizontal steam winder.

The seams worked at Coegnant were the Two Feet Nine, the Lower Six Feet, and the Upper Nine Feet, with the Lower Nine Feet the last seam to be worked. For many years the coal was conveyed to the pit bottom by electrically-powered haulage and compressed air. One 500 hp electrical main and tail haulage engine was situated near the bottom of the pit. There was also an endless rope haulage driven by a 50hp engine operating over a distance of 4,200ft from the pit bottom.

Originally Coegnant Colliery shared its take area with adjoining Caerau and St. Johns collieries, but by the 1970s operations were to the west of the Penycastell fault which runs through the Llynfi Valley causing drops of up to 600ft, which resulted in bringing the Six Feet seam opposite the Five

A vertical three cylinder haulage engine, made by Sheppards of Bridgend, found in the workings at Coegnant.

Feet seam. By the late 1970s the average length of a face at Coegnant Colliery was over 400ft, and it was on one of these faces that the colliery became one of the first mines in South Wales to operate two ranging drum shearers on the same face.

The NCB drove a 3,720ft long underground roadway in a attempt to find additional reserves in the Lower Nine Feet seam. In 1980 Coegnant miners drove through 837ft of hard rock and 552ft through coal to open up a coalface, to replace a face which had to be closed due to unusually severe geological conditions. This new face and the 1420ft of new road were driven in just nine weeks. The new face worked the 3 ft thick Yard seam with a plough with powered roof supports removed from nearby Y 1 coalface.

Mr Ron Williams, NCB Deputy Director Mining, said "Historically the geology for Coegnant doesn't look favourable, but everyone put wholehearted effort into this last attempt to make a go of it, and we can only hope it will succeed."

The colliery closed in 1981.

Above: The colliery in the rain in 1978.

Above: The colliery yard in 1981.

Above: The lamp room in 1981.

Above: Taking home tools prior to closure in 1981.

The afternoon shift waiting to descend in 1981.

The clean pit bank in 1981.

Above: A prop and bar face with a small fault in the background, 1978.
The bars were set in straight lines with at least two supports under each bar.
The photograph shows the supports prior to the shearer working the coal.

Left: A chain hauled shearer at work in poor conditions on a prop and bar face, Coegnant Colliery, 1978. Note the timber and additional steel work needed to hold the roof.

CWMGWILI AND LINDSEY COLLIERIES
CROSSHANDS, CARMARTHEN

Twin drifts were driven into the Big Vein seam around 1960, but by 1972 a £150,000 scheme merged the two mines, and despite severe geological conditions it produced an extremely high tonnage of anthracite with a work force of only 379 men. The annual output was around 126,000 tonnes of anthracite in the late 1970s.

This colliery was one of the few mines to operate a system of production headings or stalls using Joy Loaders into the 1980s. The mine appears in the British Coal list of colliery closures as having closed in 1980, but the mine was working under the ownership of Coal Investments plc until a management buy-out in 1994. The mine appears to have worked little or no coal after 1994, and was certainly closed in 1995.

A recently completed drivage in Cwmgwili Mine in 1978.

Above: The afternoon shift wait for their ride at the entrance of the mine in 1978.

Opposite page: A Joy Loader about to enter a stall; this was the last mine in South Wales to use these machines.

The Joy Loader and operator ready to commence work, 1978.

The Cwmtillery pits were sunk by John Russell in 1850. Shafts No. 2 and No. 3 date from 1850; shaft No. 1 was sunk in 1858. In 1864 the colliery was acquired by the South Wales Colliery Co., which in 1888 granted a lease of the pits to Lancaster, Spier & Co. This lease was surrendered in 1891 and a new lease granted to Lancasters Steam Coal Collieries Ltd., who in 1916 acquired all the assets of the South Wales Colliery Co. The Cwmtillery pits were owned by Lancasters Steam Coal Co. Ltd. until 1947.

Approximately 32 million tons of coal were raised at Cwmtillery between 1850 and 1950. The highest daily output was 2,085 tons on 25 May 1911; the highest weekly output 11,725 tons also in May 1911.

During the 130 years of its life, methods of working had changed. Originally the pillar and stall method was used, later this was changed to longwall heading and stall and longwall Barry system. Cwmtillery was one of the first collieries in South Wales to use the Meco-Moore Power Loader. In 1977 the longest manriding installation in South Wales was commissioned to transport men and materials 9,300ft into the Garw seam. After a life of 132 years the colliery closed in 1982.

Depth of shafts:

No. 1 shaft 2,349ft to Old Coal seam.
No. 2 shaft 1,665ft to Black Vein.
No. 3 shaft 2,160ft to Old Coal seam.

Wooden headframes at Cwmtillery c1910

Above: Decorative brick work on the fan, most likely a Walker Fan.

Below: Pit head at Cwmtillery, with the baths on the left of the picture taken in 1980.

Opposite page: The pit bottom in 1979.

CYNHEIDRE COLLIERY
PONTYATES, CARMARTHEN

The colliery stood on the flanks of the Gwendraeth Fawr valley some 4 miles north of Llanelli. The two shafts were completed and the pit commenced working around 1966; these shafts were linked to another shaft sunk in 1939 and the Pentremawr Slant. Earlier slants of around 1870s existed at Pentremawr which were soon abandoned as they struck faults which rendered the anthracite unworkable.

The NCB had estimated that the colliery would have a workable reserve of 60 million tonnes of high grade anthracite, but the colliery was sunk in the most geologically disturbed conditions in the South Wales coalfield. Between October 1962 and 1971 67 outbursts were recorded, but fortunately none resulted in any loss of life until 6 April 1971, when a major outburst of coal and firedamp killed six men with 69 others suffered varying degrees of asphyxia. At the time of the outburst the combined colliery produced about 20,000 tonnes of coal annually and employed 1,178 men underground and 422 on the surface.

Although as many as eight seams had been worked at Cynheidre, by 1979 only the Big seam was worked at a depth of 1,980ft, although it was planned to drive in to the Pumpquart seam which was over 600ft below the Big Vein, but had reserves of more than 12 million tonnes.

An NCB press release dated 26 February 1986 stated "that the Board had approved investment of £30 million to mine rich new reserves of anthracite to secure mining jobs at Cynheidre Colliery well into the next century." With the new Carway Fawr development, the investment in South Wales stood at £80 million that year.

In spite of this massive investment the colliery closed in January 1989.

Left: Empty mine cars waiting near pit bottom in 1978.

Opposite page: Cynheidre Colliery from the air in 1978.

INTAKE ⟩

DOWNCAST SHAFT S1
950 Metres ⟩

Above: Mine cars at a loading point. Here the conveyor discharges in cars which are taken to pit bottom.

Opposite page: Onsetter at one of the 660 level, in the Cynheidre shaft. The deepest shaft was 2,368ft in depth.

A typical junction at Cynheidre where timber chocks were extensively used.

Main trunk road with high speed conveyor.

Full mine cars at the shaft on the 660ft level.

DEEP DUFFRYN COLLIERY
MOUNTAIN ASH, GLAMORGAN

The colliery was sunk at Mountain Ash on the Taff Vale Railway by David Williams of Ynyscynon in 1850; the sinking proved to be an extremely hazardous and expensive operation and cast iron tubbing was installed to hold back soft sandy material and water. The sinking to the Four Feet seam at a depth 849ft took five years to complete and was said by David Williams to have cost a "guinea an inch". Williams worked the Four Feet seam, with an output of around 150 tons per day.

The colliery was bought by John Nixon in 1857 for the sum of £42,000. Conditions in the colliery were poor by mid 19th century standards; the steam engine wound and pumped and a ventilation furnace on the second shaft provided inadequate ventilation. Nixon found the air was so heavily charged with firedamp as to be almost insupportable. Within two years Nixon had increased production to one thousand tons per day, with modern powerful winding engines, and with a ventilation machine known as Nixon's Ventilator. Nixon's Ventilator was installed about 1858 and is known to have worked for thirty years without a day's stoppage, and was only dismantled in 1937.

It was at Deep Duffryn Colliery that John Nixon first introduced into the South Wales coalfield the longwall system of working. The machine for weighing small coal, known as Billy Fairplay, made its appearance there. Another invention by John Nixon was a spiral drum where the weight of the cages was balanced, and less strain was placed on the winding engine.

The shafts of Deep Duffryn were originally sunk to the depth of 849ft to the Four Feet seam but were later deepened in 1926-27 to the Seven Feet seam at a depth of 1,146ft and in, 1955 the shaft was sunk to the Five Feet/Gellideg seam to a total depth of 1,227ft.

seams worked before 1927	seams worked after 1927
Two Feet Nine Inch seam Four Feet Six Feet Nine Feet	Yard Seven Feet Five Feet/Gellideg

The Four Feet, Six Feet, and Nine Feet seams were extensively worked, and the colliery produced one of the highest tonnages of the best quality dry steam coal in the South Wales coalfield before the World War II.

Deep Duffryn Colliery was owned and worked by the Nixons Navigation Company until the early 1920s, and was then merged with the Welsh Associated Collieries Limited. In 1935 the colliery was acquired by Powell Duffryn Ltd.

The colliery was vested in the NCB on 1 January 1947 and worked until closed in 1979.

The headframe in 1974. It was made of bull-headed railway rails bound together with wrought iron bands riveted to the rail flanges. This headframe is said to have been built in 1888.

Left: View of headframe from the east. Apart from the frame over the sheaves this headframe had not changed since it was erected in 1888.

Below left: Ventilation at Deep Duffryn Colliery was effected by Nixon's Horizontal Ventilator and two Ventilating Furnaces on the smaller upcast shaft. This photograph shows the commencement of the air passage in the shaft, taken from the roof of the cage.
This structure was built in alluvial ground and was extremely difficult to build, massive concrete beds were employed under the roads to the screens, the crown of the arch being only 3ft below the roads, the construction was found to be extremely slow and costly.

Below right: Looking back up the shaft from the roof of the cage. The cast iron tubbing was installed at the sinking in 1850.

Above: View of original cast iron tubbing, looking down the shaft in 1977-78.

Opposite page: The two pitmen inspecting the shaft from the roof of the cage in 1977-78.
Note the old style leather safety harness which was soon replaced by jacket type.
The opening of Nixon's fan drift is visible in the background above the edge of the cast iron tubbing.

Above: Typical roadway with steel arches and conveyor belt in 1977.

Left: Tail Gate of V 44s face in 1978.

Opposite page: Powered supports and shearer on V 44s face in the Gellideg seam in 1978.

The stump of the old pumping engine house which was used as a base for the backstays of the headframe. It is not known when the beam pumping engine became disused. It was clearly a beam working pump rods through a bell crank, for the engine was some distance from the shaft.

Nixon's Ventilator

Drawings of the Nixon's Ventilator made by the company in 1898. This ventilator had pistons of which the centre piece was cast iron 3ft by 2ft 9in. The piston was made of a double skin $3/8$ in. near the centre and $1/4$ in. thick on the outer edge. The piston, which was six tons in weight, was carried on two rails and worked up to 12 strokes per minute at seven feet stroke which gave 221,760 cubic feet of air per minute.

NIXON'S VENTILATOR
AT NAVIGATION COLLIERY.

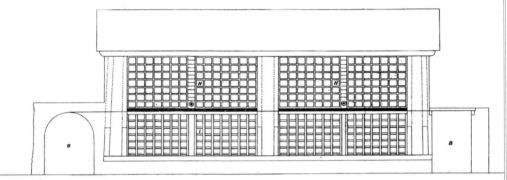

ELEVATION

From Proceedings S.Wales Institute of Engineering 1867 vol5.

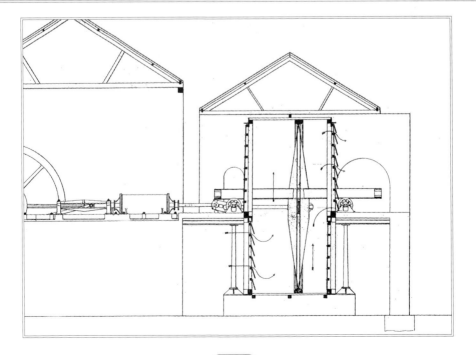

DEEP NAVIGATION COLLIERY
TREHARRIS, GLAMORGAN

This mine was one of the deepest and best equipped collieries in South Wales, sunk over the 1872 -1878 period, and originally known as Harris Navigation. The No. 1 shaft was the downcast with a diameter of 17ft and a depth of 1,947ft to the Four Feet seam. The No.2 shaft was also 17ft in diameter and 2,157ft in depth to the Six Feet seam. Both shafts were lined throughout with firebricks, the thickness varying from 9in. to 18in.

Everything at Harris Navigation was bigger and better than most other pits at the time of sinking. The Cornish pumping engine was built by the Perran Foundry, in 1875. The cylinder had a diameter of 100in., and an 11ft stroke. The cylinder was steam - jacketed and enclosed with $4\frac{1}{2}$in. brickwork. Water was raised in 7 lifts of pumps from a depth of 2,010ft, these lifts being worked by seven rams. The pump rods ranged from 16in. to 8in. square.

The winding engine was made by John Fowler & Co. in 1878 and had two inverted cylinders 54in. in diameter and 7ft stroke, with Cornish valves and a drum of spiral form of 32ft diameter. The headgear on the downcast shaft was of wrought iron and was 81ft in height from the surface to the centre of the pulleys.

The massive engine houses for the vertical winder and the smaller house for the 100in. Cornish pump together with the head frame was a spectacular scene when viewed from the south. The winding engine of the No.2 shaft, the upcast, had two horizontal cylinders of 42in. diameter with a 6ft stroke.

Prior to World War I two seams were worked, the Four Feet and the Six Feet. These seams were worked by the longwall system entirely, both by the South Wales method, with 33ft stalls, and by the Nottingham system with a breadth of stall varying from 90 to 120ft. At this time no explosives were used to bring down coal, but Ammonite was used occasionally in ripping the gateways.

For most of its life the pit was owned by the Ocean Coal Company and it continued to turn a very substantial annual tonnage of high quality coal. After Nationalisation the pit worked the Seven Feet seam to the west, and the Lower Nine Feet seam to the east.

Two years after the centenary celebrations the colliery recorded the best ever profit of £2.6 million and in the second week of May 1981 the 780 men hit a productivity record of 3.10 tonnes per man shift. The total saleable output for the week was 9,750 tonnes.

In 1985 the colliery was equipped with one of the most expensive and massive powered supports which weighed up to 18 tonnes, and the face when in production could cut up to 1500 tonnes of coal in one day. During the first week in March the high-technology face cut a saleable output of 9,000 tonnes, with a coal face productivity reaching 28 tonnes per man shift. By March 1986 the colliery production reached half a million tonnes of saleable coal for the year.

The colliery closed in 1991 after a life of 112 years.

The driver's position and indicator on the original vertical winding engine, c.1880.

The recently completed colliery in 1878 The main building is the engine house for the vertical winder, with the engine house of the 100in. pumping engine on the right of the picture.
The figure on the left is the colliery policeman.

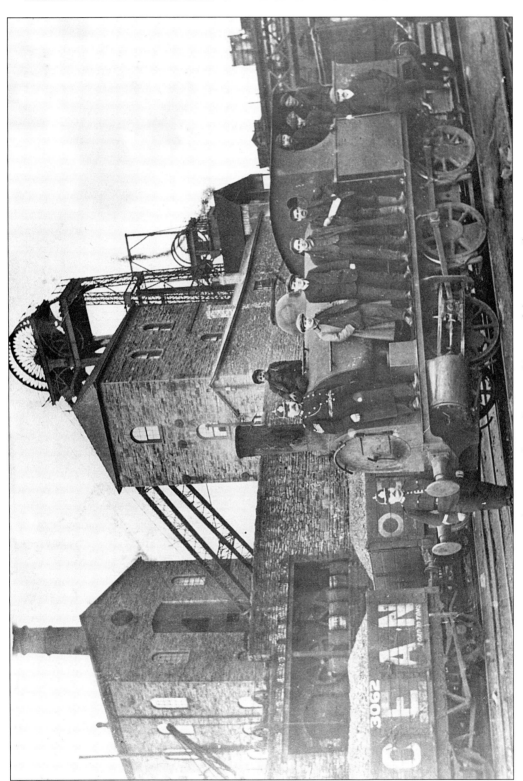

A 0-6-0 tank engine with a police guard in one of the many strikes.

Above: A view of the pithead in 1978, taken just before the surface reorganisation.

Left: The downcast headframe erected in 1877-78; this was one of the most striking of all South Wales headframes and when completed one of the deepest shafts in the coalfield.

The Pit bottom downcast shaft in 1978.

Anderson Strathclyde shearer at work on a face with powered supports.

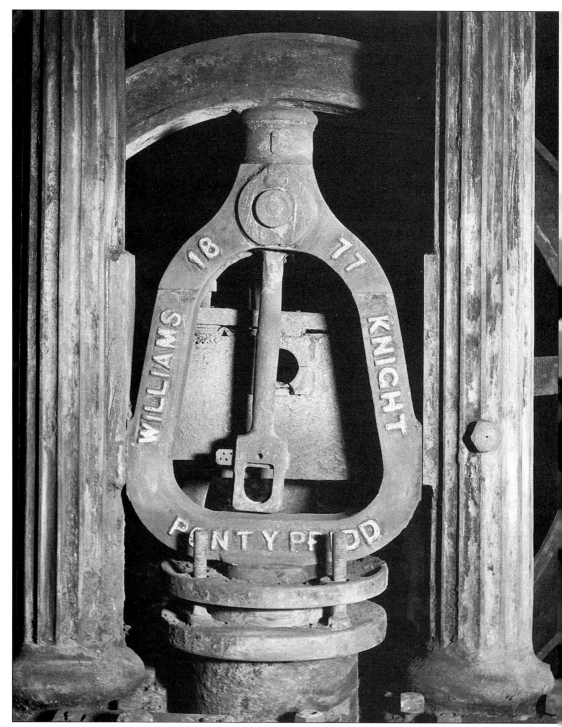

Old Steam pump made by Williams Knight of Pontyprydd.

Fernhill Colliery was originally sunk to the Upper Four Feet seam in 1869 by Ebenezer Lewis, who also sank the United National Collieries, at Wattstown in the Rhondda Fach. Fernhill was situated on the extreme northern end of the Rhondda Fawr, two and a half miles to the north of Treherbert station. At the time of the sinking, the Earl of Dunraven was the owner of the mineral rights.

North Dunraven Colliery, an earlier sinking, 900ft to the north west of Fernhill, was acquired and linked to Fernhill about 1893. The Fernhill shafts were oval in section and were completed as far as the Upper Four Feet seam in 1869. The No. 1 shaft, the downcast, was 17ft 6in. by 11ft 6in.. The No. 2, the upcast shaft, was 132ft to the south of the No. 1 shaft. No. 2 was 16 ft by 11 ft in section. Fernhill did not appear to have worked for two years in 1877-78 as it does not appear in the Mines Inspectors' list of mines then.

The Colliery proprietors were listed as Messrs George Watkinson and Sons of Halifax, and the company was known as the United Collieries. Around 1893 the United Collieries purchased the Dunraven Colliery, which was then linked underground to Fernhill Colliery, and the company was then known as the Fernhill Collieries Ltd. with shafts numbered 1 to 4.

At the turn of the century only the Gorllwyn, Two Feet Nine, the Yard and Six Feet seams were worked, each seam producing a high-class smokeless steam coal. The No. 2 Rhondda seam was also worked by levels in the hillside some 192ft above the shafts.

All coal was worked on the longwall system, in the Two Feet Nine Inch seam and in the Gorllwyn seam, the stalls were driven 42ft wide from the rise headings, the gate-roads being cut off at 150ft. In the Yard and Six Feet seams the stalls were driven 33ft wide, and horses were only used to take the trams each way between the face and the engine roads. The coal was brought down chiefly from pressure wedging assisted by plain wedges, and the only explosive used was Roburite which was used in ripping stall roads and stone drifts.

In 1910 J.W. Beynon and Fernhill Collieries amalgamated, and 6 years later the colliery was raising 500,000 tons of coal per year. In 1920 the Company sank the No.5 shaft on the site of the Old Dunraven Colliery which then became known as Fernhill Colliery. The Colliery later came under the ownership of the Powell Duffryn Group, where it remained until Nationalisation in 1947.

In 1967 Fernhill and Tower Collieries linked underground to form a single unit employing 860 men, who produced about 250,000 tons of coal per year. This colliery was one of the last pits in South Wales to work a longwall timber face with the Anderson Boyes AB15 undercutting machine, but this method of production was phased out in the mid 1970s. This shaft was also the last in the South Wales coalfield to use clapper boards. These were timber covers which prevented air from leaking into the shaft—especially an upcast shaft. In the final years of the mine the Five Feet and Nine Feet seams were worked by ranging drum shearers and hydraulic chock supports, turning around 7500 tonnes of coal per week.

A fine horizontal twin cylinder steam winding engine by Leighs of Patricroft, Lancashire, was used operationally, running on compressed air until cut up in the early 1980s.

The colliery finally ceased working in 1980.

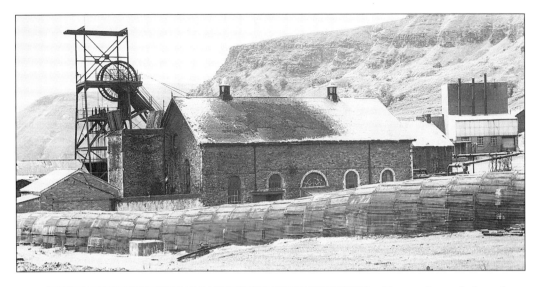

Above: General view of Fernhill Colliery in the mid 1970s. The structure in the foreground was built to protect the men when returning from the pithead to the baths in the winter, which can be severe in the upper reaches of the Rhondda.

The large building in the centre of the picture housed generators with the fan at the eastern end.

Left: Steam winder built by Leighs of Patricroft in the 1870s. The cylinders were 27in in diameter with a 5ft 6in stroke.

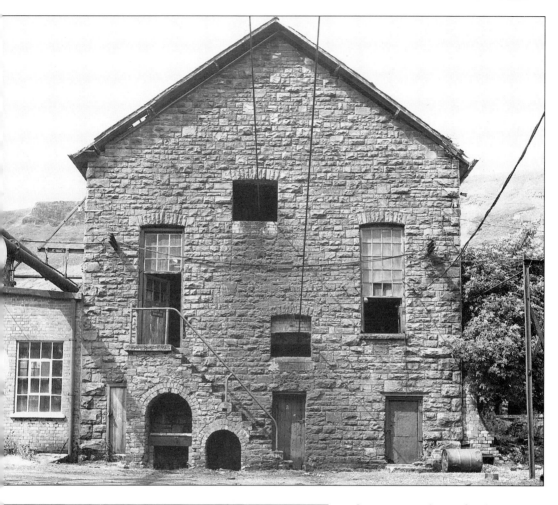

Above: Engine house for the Leigh winding engine in 1973.

Left: Clapper boards over the No.3 shaft. This was the last pit in South Wales to use clapper boards. This system was also in use the Somerset Coalfield at Kilmersdon Colliery until closure in 1973.

The pit bottom on the No.5 shaft, in 1978.

Right: The jib of an A B 15 Hydraulic undercutter on a timbered longwall face.

Below: One of the last rubber conveyor belt on the timbered face, 1974.

Stable hole on a previous face. The stable hole allowed the shearer to be moved forward and commence a new cut.

Repair work underway in a gate road. Note the extensive stone dusting which will prevent any explosion from spreading.

Large Gullick chocks and an Anderson Strathclyde shearer with water spray, 1978.

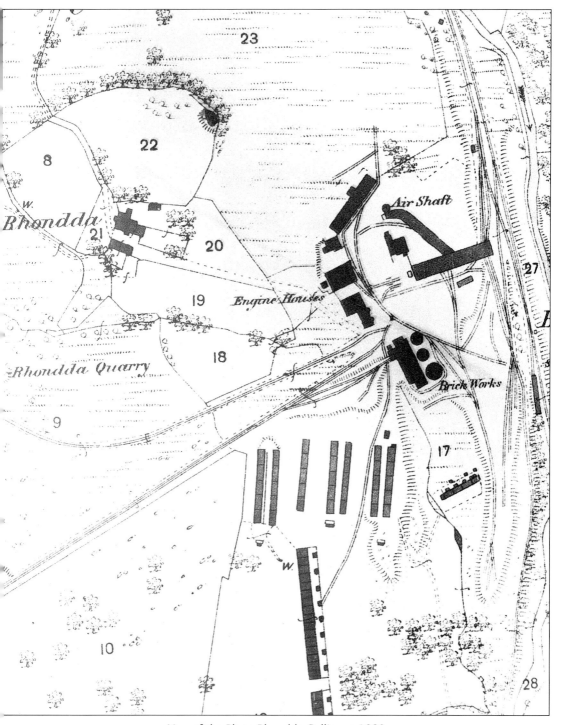

Map of the Blaen-Rhondda Colliery c.1880.

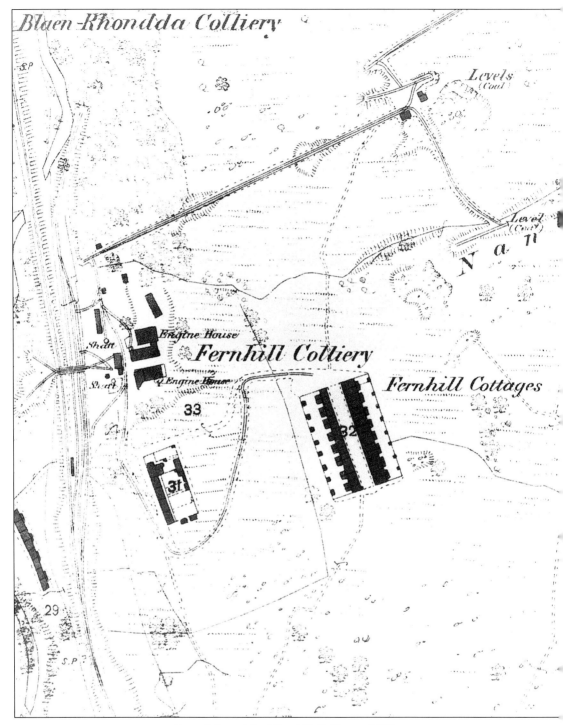

Map of the original Fernhill Colliery c.1880.

Garw Colliery, situated in the Garw Valley, was sunk by the Ocean Coal Company in 1883; two shafts were sunk 144ft apart. The downcast shaft was 15ft in diameter, the upcast shaft 14ft in diameter, both shafts being just over 1,150ft in depth.

Ffaldau Colliery was sunk in 1877 by Ffaldau Collieries which worked the pit until it was acquired by Cory Brothers in 1934, who in turn sold it to the Powell Duffryn Group in 1942. When the NCB took over the mine at Vesting Day the colliery was reconstructed and an extremely high output figure achieved in subsequent years.

The two mines were linked in 1975 and coal was raised at the Garw end. The colliery take at this period was just over five square miles working the lower Nine Feet and the Gellideg seams, the combined units producing 240,000 tonnes of coal a year. The colliery had an estimated reserve of 7½ million tons of coal and a drilling programme was expected to increase the reserve.

The B1 coal face was abandoned in the winter of 1985, because of worsening physical conditions, and the colliery depended on M7 face with one other face under development. The colliery had to achieve an output of 7,500 tonnes per week to break even, unfortunately this figure was not obtained and the colliery closed at the end of 1985.

Ffaldau Colliery from the main road in Pontycymer, 1973.

Pit head at Ffaldau Colliery in 1977. The colliery was linked to Garw Colliery where all was raised, the Ffaldau surface being retained for ventilation and a second exit.

A new Gullick shield chock installation at Garw Colliery in 1977-8; the seam thickness was 6ft.

Right: The pit bottom of Garw Colliery in 1977.

Opposite page: General view of Garw Colliery with village in background 1977.

Graig Merthyr Colliery was said to have been driven in 1868 and the adjacent mine Cefn Drim in 1910. Graigola Merthyr was possibly driven by Frank Yeo and Thomas Cory who later formed the Graigola Merthyr Company Ltd. The colliery worked the Graigola seam, the Swansea Six Feet and Three Feet seams, and about 605 men worked at the mine producing around 150,000 tonnes of coal, but the mine closed due to exhaustion of reserves in 1978.

Until closure the output of the mine was worked down the Graig Merthyr Valley by steam locomotives *Austerity* 2765 and *Norma*, to the washery at Brynlliw Colliery.

Entrance to the drift mine with a journey of empty trams being lowered by cable haulage into the mine, in 1977.

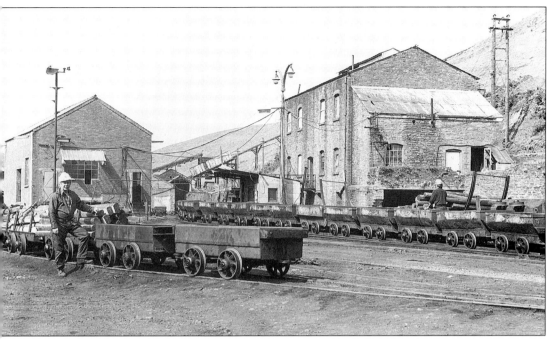

Above: The colliery yard in 1977 with a long journey of trams waiting to be run into the mine. In the foreground are special cut-down trams used for moving supplies.

Above: Empty trams on a warm summer's day, the entrance to the old Cefn Drim slant can be seen on the extreme left of the picture.

Austerity 2765 working a coal train down the Graig Merthyr valley to the washery in 1977.

The most surprising feature of Graig Merthyr Colliery was the unsupported sandstone roof. The roof of the Graigola Seam was exceptionally strong, this mine and Clydach Merthyr Slant were the only mines operated by the National Coal Board to work with a roof which needed little or no support.

A 20ft wide unsupported roof at Graig Merthyr in 1977.

LADY WINDSOR/
ABERCYNON COLLIERY
ABERCYNON, GLAMORGAN

Abercynon Colliery was sunk between 1890-1896 by the Dowlais Iron Company which sank a pair of shafts 20ft in diameter to the Nine Feet seam at a depth of 2,220ft. Around 1900, the pit was acquired by Guest Keen & Nettlefold Ltd. who later employed more than 2,500 men. By 1930 the pit was sold to Welsh Associated Collieries who were soon taken over by the Powell Duffryn Group.

The pumping was originally undertaken by a Hathorn Davey & Co. tandem horizontal compound and condensing engine with a high pressure cylinder 45in. in diameter, and the low pressure cylinder 78in. in diameter with a 10ft stroke. There were two piston rods to the high pressure cylinder, joined by a cross-head. A connecting-rod from the latter moved the pump rods by two quadrants placed over the side of the shaft.

Unfortunately all traces of this engine had disappeared by the 1970s. There were also three direct-acting steam pumps made by Messrs Pearn & Co. in three lodges in the shaft. I recorded the middle pump in the 1970s which was placed 1,005ft down. It had two horizontal cylinders 22in. in diameter an 18in. stroke, and two 10in. rams; the rising main was 9in. in diameter. These pumps were capable of forcing the whole of the water to the surface should the main pump require any repairs.

The headgear of Abercynon Colliery was very impressive, and stood 100ft high, the backstays were extremely long and were most likely the longest in South Wales with a length of 175ft.

The colliery was linked with Lady Windsor Colliery at Inysybwl in the 1970s.

Lady Windsor Colliery was sunk on land owned by Lord Windsor. The sinking commenced in 1884 and was completed after 20 months work. The downcast shaft was 19ft in diameter and 1,680ft to the Four Feet seam, and 1,800ft to the lower loading stage in a lower seam. The upcast shaft was 246ft distant to the west and 17ft in diameter, and 1,860ft in depth including 60ft of sump. After the sinking, 619 men and boys were employed underground with 80 horses.

In 1974 two parallel tunnels were driven under the mountain separating the two collieries. This was the commencement of a £500,000 project to link the two collieries forming a single unit raising all coal at Lady Windsor for washing and blending. High speed conveyors under remote control from Lady Windsor carried the coal into a new 400 tonnes spiral bunker shaft, the first of its kind in any British coalfield. The combined unit worked an area of around 6 square miles, bounded on the east by the Werfa fault and on the west by the Ty Mawr fault. The geological conditions within the take were amongst the worst in South Wales, yet the pit was able to win annually a quarter of a million tonnes of coal from the Nine Feet, Seven Feet, Bute and Five Feet/Gellideg seams. In 1980 the estimated workable reserves were almost 20 million tonnes.

The colliery closed in 1988.

On the sign:
WERFA RETURN DRIVAGE
ONLY 17 MEN ALLOWED
IN THIS DRIVAGE AT ANY
ONE TIME.
MANAGER

Above: The undermanager inspecting hardwood chocks at the entrance to the Werfa drivage in Abercynon Colliery, 1977.

Left: The massive headframes of Abercynon Colliery in 1974. Painted blue, for many years they were a landmark on the Merthyr to Cardiff Road. The back stays were said to be the longest in the coalfield.

A Steam locomotive in the yard of Lady Windsor Colliery during the winter of 1977, with the upcast shaft in the background.

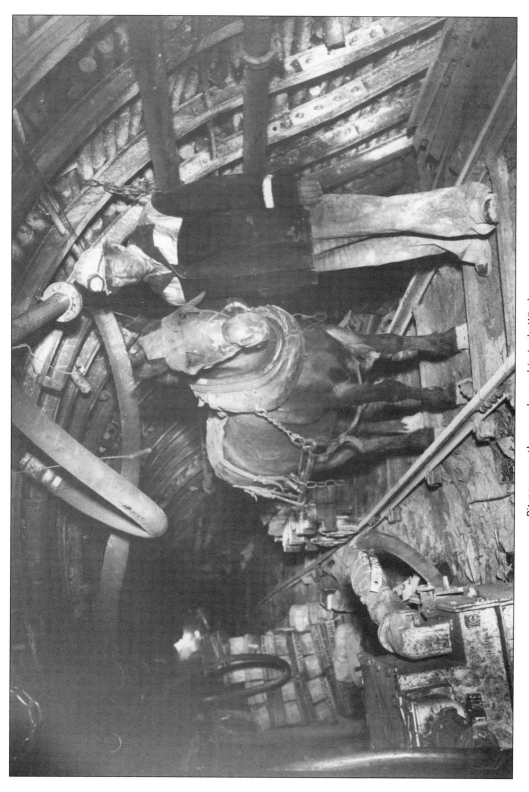

Pit pony on the supply road in Lady Windsor.

A plough on a low seam at Lady Windsor Colliery.

Recently installed skip in the pit bottom. The shaft did not stop at this point but terminated in a sump 60 or 80ft below the landing.

The pit bottom in 1977 before modernisation, with empty trams on a creeper.

Above: This and the next plate show the middle of the three Pearn direct-acting steam pumps which were situated in lodges in the shaft.

Left: This pump could only be reached by descending the shaft on the top of the skip, chained to the winding cable.

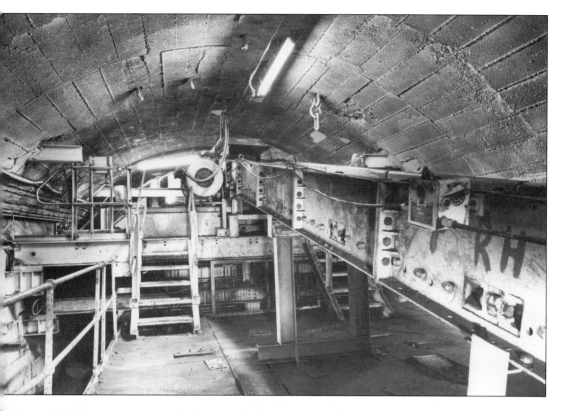

Above: The newly reconstructed pit bottom at Lady Windsor.

Left: Fitters at work in the reconstructed pit bottom prior to the fitting of the skips.

In 1850 brothers David and John Thomas leased the mineral rights of Hafod Fach and Nyth-Bran farms on the eastern bank of the river Rhondda just below Porth. When the brothers reached the No. 3 Rhondda seam they found it too thin to work. Not discouraged, they deepened the shaft to try to work the Hafod seam, but they unfortunately hit a fault, and, having spent over £30,000, the Thomas brothers abandoned the project. Also in 1850 Edward Mills had sunk the Coedcae Colliery on the south bank of the river, but this soon encountered water problems and was also abandoned. Later the Thomas brothers tried reworking the Coedcae Colliery, but again water became a problem and the colliery was abandoned for the second time.

The Coedcae Colliery was working in the early 1870s and traded under the name Coedcae Coal Company, the Hafod Pit reappears in the Mines Inspectors' Reports in 1881. Until 1893 it worked the bituminous coals; after this date the deeper steam coals were worked until the reorganisation under Powell Duffryn in the 1930s. The Coedcae only worked the upper bituminous seams. It was closed by the mid 1930s, and after this date both shafts were retained for pumping purposes only.

Sometime in the mid 1870s William Thomas Lewis (later Lord Merthyr) purchased the Hafod and Coedcae collieries, the concern being known as Lewis Merthyr. By 1880, W. T. Lewis had sunk the Bertie shaft; the Trefor followed some ten years later. In 1881 the colliery was known as Lewis Merthyr Navigation Collieries Limited, but by 1900 the concern was registered as Lewis Merthyr Consolidated Collieries Limited. By 1900 the five pits were producing almost a million tons of coal annually.

Winding shafts, 4 in number, had a combined output of 20,000 tons weekly. The main winding engine had a pair of 42in. cylinders with a 6ft stroke, and a spiral drum ranging from 15ft to 30ft in diameter. $17^3/_4$ engine strokes raised the cage to the landing, the operation of winding and changing occupying 1 minute 10 seconds. Ventilation was by a Schiele fan, 13ft 6in. in diameter, producing 230,000 cubic ft of air per minute. At the surface was a compound haulage engine with cylinders of 14 and 24in., working an endless-rope haulage plane of 5,400ft from the pit bottom. The engine was geared 13 to 1 and there were frequently from 60 to 80 trams carrying 28 cwts of coal each being hauled at the same time. The quantity of coal hauled varied from 800 to 1,100 tons per day. Twelve haulage engines of various sizes worked by compressed air, and from 140 to 180 horses were also engaged in the haulage of coal.

By World War I, the coal was worked on the longwall system with coal-cutting machines at work in some seams. In the Hafod seam, cutters of the bar type, disc type, and chain type were used, all driven by compressed air. In the years before World War I, the output of the company was approximately 1,500,000 tons per year. A mile to the north-east, in the Rhondda Fach, the Lady Lewis Colliery was sunk in 1904; then, in 1905, Lewis Merthyr Consolidated Collieries acquired the Universal Colliery at Senghenydd, later to suffer the worst mining disaster in British coal mining history. In 1929, Powell Duffryn took over operations and that same year Coedcae stopped winding coal. Hafod No. 2 followed in 1930, and in 1933 the Hafod No. 1 ceased also. In 1935, Powell Duffryn and the Welsh Associated Collieries (1929) amalgamated to form Powell Duffryn Associated Collieries and became the largest coal-producing group in the world. After amalgamation, manpower and production at Lewis Merthyr slowly contracted so that by 1937 only 1,070 men worked underground with 212 men on the surface. By Vesting Day in 1947, manpower had climbed to 1,428 men underground and 303

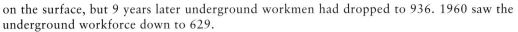

on the surface, but 9 years later underground workmen had dropped to 936. 1960 saw the underground workforce down to 629.

In the 1950s the following seams were worked in descending order: Two Feet Nine, Six Feet and Gellideg.

On 22 November 1956, gas in a roadhead cavity was ignited by a fall of stone in the N 4 district in the Two Feet Nine seam. Two men were killed outright, seven men later died of their injuries, and five other men were also injured. The manager, Mr Fox, was one of the men who later died in hospital, At the time of the explosion the colliery was producing around 1,250 tons of coal per day, with 936 men underground and 226 on the surface.

In 1958 Lewis Merthyr and Tymawr were merged. All coalwinding at Lewis Merthyr ceased as Tymawr was used for coaling, with materials going down Lewis Merthyr. In May 1969, Edward Withey was appointed Agent Manager of the combined mines of Tymawr and Lewis Merthyr.

Lewis Merthyr/Tymawr had been operating as a combined unit for some 15 years working the Four Feet, and Upper Nine Feet but, as the productive Four Feet seam approached the end of its life, attempts were made to work the Upper Nine Feet seam with a fully mechanised coalface. Both seams above and below the Upper Nine Feet had been worked, and this resulted in conditions which made the use of powered supports almost impossible. In January 1983, the N 92 face consumed one tonne of timber for every 10 tonnes of coal produced. Production came to an end on 14 March 1983 with production continuing in the Four Feet seam until July, when coaling ceased for ever at Lewis Merthyr and Tymawr.

Lewis Merthyr Colliery is now known as the Rhondda Heritage Centre which opened in 1989, but unfortunately only the Bertie and Trefor Pits now survive, two thirds of the Lewis Merthyr Colliery complex having completely disappeared. The Coedcae Pit and the two shafts of the Hafod Nos. 1 & 2 pits, the baths, workshops, boiler house and timber yard have all gone apart from the heapstead of the No. 1 Hafod Pit with its date stone of 1870 and the initials of the Lewis Merthyr Navigation.

Over page top: Lewis Merthyr in the early years of the last century. The Coedcae or house coal pit is situated to the right of the coke ovens, with the two Hafod pits on the north bank of the river. The complex had working 5 shafts and a large battery of coke ovens. Only the Bertie and Trefor pit heads now remain, a fraction of the original complex.

Over page bottom: The Lewis Merthyr Complex from Cwm George around 1900. The Trefor, Bertie and Coedcae shafts are to the left of the picture with the Hafod No.1 on the extreme right. In the middle distance can be seen the abandoned headframe of the old Llwyncelyn Colliery.

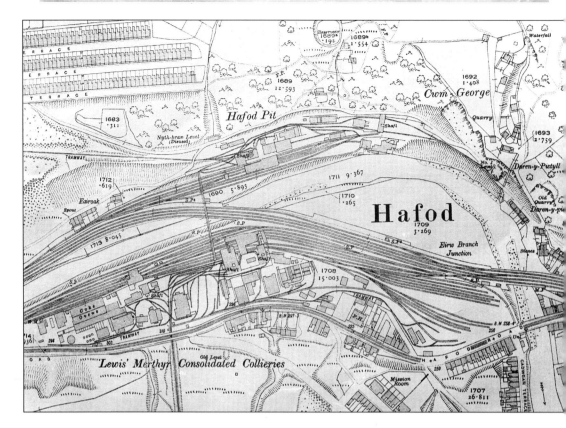

Above: The morning shift, March 1983.

Above: The Coedcae shaft and engine house.

Above: The pit head baths in 1983, the powder store was situated behind the baths.

Left: The wooden headframe of the Coedcae or house coal pit with the spare cage on the right.

The pit head at Lewis Merthyr in 1982. The colliery ceased coaling in July 1983.

The pit bottom of the Bertie shaft in 1983. No coal winding had taken place at Lewis Merthyr since 1958, all coal was raised at Tymawr Colliery.

Chocks standing in the yard waiting to be taken underground in 1977.

Idris Reed, overman, testing for gas with a Thomas & Williams Garforth lamp on the 416s face, 29 April 1983.

Tom Neate at work on the North 91 face in 1978.

The 416s was the last face at Lewis Merthyr Colliery. Here it may be seen with chain haulage for shearer and Gullick Dobson chocks.

Props and bars with a chain hauled shearer on the North 91s face in the 9ft seam in 1978. This was an extremely fine face.

MARDY COLLIERY
RHONDDA FACH, GLAMORGAN

The original Mardy Colliery known as No. 1 and No. 2 was sunk by Mordecai Jones and Wheatly Cobb both natives of Brecon, and the first coal was raised in 1876. Shafts 1 and 2 were originally sunk to the Abergorki seam, but when the colliery was acquired by Locketts Merthyr Company in 1877, the shafts were deepened to the Upper Four Feet seam, and then at a later date deepened to the Five Feet seam. An interesting feature of the sinking was that very little water was encountered, so no pumping appliances were needed.

The No. 1 shaft, the upcast, was 16ft in diameter, and was 1,155ft deep to the Five Feet seam. The downcast shaft, No.2 was situated 99ft to the north of the No. 1 shaft, the depth and diameter of both shafts being the same. The output of coal in 1895 from the No. 1 and No. 2 shafts was about 1200 tons for nine hours work. It would appear that in the No. 1 shaft the working of coal was confined to the Five Feet and the Abergorki seams, the latter being a locomotive coal. In the No. 2 shaft the Two Feet Nine, Upper Four Feet, and Six Feet were all worked by the longwall system, the stalls were 42ft wide, with a gateway in the middle of each, the back workings being filled up with refuse stone and small coal.

On 23 December 1885 a tragic underground explosion killed 81 men; it was probably caused by a Comet lamp (a naked light lamp) igniting firedamp. William Thomas was awarded the Medal for Valour for leading the rescue operation.

It was thought that Mardy was the first pit in South Wales to use electricity for pumping, for electric pumps were installed in 1881. The dynamo produced a current of 220 amperes at 110 volts, the motor was made at the colliery and was placed in the Abergorki seam, three quarters of a mile from the shaft. The engine which drove the pump dynamo also drove a dynamo which produced lighting for the pit bottoms of No. 1 and No. 2 shafts, and the main roads for a distance of 600ft, also the underground stables and engine houses.

The horizontal steam winding engine on the No. 1 shaft had 32in. cylinders, with a 5ft stroke, Cornish valve gear, and a cast-iron cylindrical drum 14ft in diameter. The engine raised one tram in each cage; the average weight of coal carried in a tram was about 30 cwt. The engine of the No. 2 shaft was a duplicate of the engine on the No. 2 shaft. In 1878 a Waddle fan was erected on the No. 1 shaft, with a diameter of 45ft and could pass 220,000 cubic feet of air per minute.

The No.3 Pit around 1905.

No.3 and 4 Pits after the last war and before the extensive modernisation.
The chimney on the hillside was connected to the boilers and was built high-up to provide extra draught for the boilers.

The Mardy No. 3 pit was sunk by Locketts Merthyr Colliery Company Ltd in 1893. It was connected to their workings which had already reached the area from the older Nos. 1 and 2 shafts about one mile to the south east. This shaft was sunk to 45ft below the Gellideg seam at a total depth of 1,500ft.

The main coal landing was from the Bute seam at a depth of 1,284ft. In 1914 the No. 4 shaft was sunk to the Six Feet seam and used as an upcast for the Six Feet workings from No. 1 shaft and No. 2 shaft and coal winding from the Gorllwyn seam.

In 1932 Locketts Merthyr was acquired by the Welsh Associated Collieries who then worked the Yard, Nine Feet, and a small portion of the Seven Feet seam; work was then suspended in 1934. Meanwhile the No. 4 pit was deepened to the Bute seam to act as an upcast for the No. 3 shaft workings.

After suspension of coal production in 1934, a new drift 1,200ft long was driven to the Six Feet seam intersecting the Nine Feet seam. During the driving, the colliery passed into the hands of the Powell Duffryn Collieries who recommenced working the Six Feet and Nine Feet seams.

Coal production continued until October 1940 when it was suspended due to the reduced demand as a result of the fall of France. But from 1940 to 1946 about 30 tons of coal a month were raised to supply the boilers for maintenance and pumping.

In 1948 the NCB approved a £4 million reconstruction project to reopen and reconstruct the Nos. 3 and 4 shafts at Mardy to work the massive coal reserves at the northern end of the Rhondda Fach and Cwmdare Valley. The colliery layout was changed considerably, and all of the original structures were demolished and rebuilt with concrete, brick and glass. New engine houses were built at an angle of 90 degrees to the old buildings. The entire pit was reconstructed with new washery, canteen, pithead baths, lamp room and offices all built in the new cubic style, the only fragment of the old pit being the chimney up on the hillside which was pulled down around 1980-82.

Mardy Pit in 1977; the massive brick structure built over the
railway sidings is the washery.

Underground roads were driven through the mountain from Mardy to link with Bwllfa No. 1 which continued to be used for ventilation only. In 1957 Bwllfa No. 2 closed and the men were transferred to Mardy; later men were also moved from the Ferndale Pits which had closed in 1959.

The horizon method of mining was employed after reconstruction, and it was suggested that as many as 12 seams could be worked, as they were relatively flat. Standard three-ton mine cars were drawn by locomotives and the trains consisted of 35 cars. It was thought that reserves worked from the Mardy development could be 120 million tons of coal which would last more than 100 years.

The final mining programme worked the Yard and Five Feet/Gellideg seams from five miles of underground roadway, and more than two miles of high speed conveyors. The colliery worked an area of around three square miles, bounded on the north west by the 125ft Hirwaun fault, and on the west by the 170ft 6in. fault. On the far side lay the workings of the neighbouring Tower /Fernhill Colliery, beneath the Rhigos mountain between Hirwaun and the Rhondda Fawr.

The pit produced about 200,000 tons of top quality dry steam coal, for the Phurnacite Plant at Abercwmboi.

On 30 June 1986 the last tram of coal was raised at Mardy, and all coal worked there was later raised at Tower Colliery through an underground connection. Six years later British Coal closed Mardy ending 177 years of deep mining in the Rhondda Valley

Empty mine cars waiting at the pit top; each car could hold three tons.

Above: John Bates the lampman passing a Garforth lamp to Deputy John (Jackie) Davies.

Left: The pit bank around 1980.

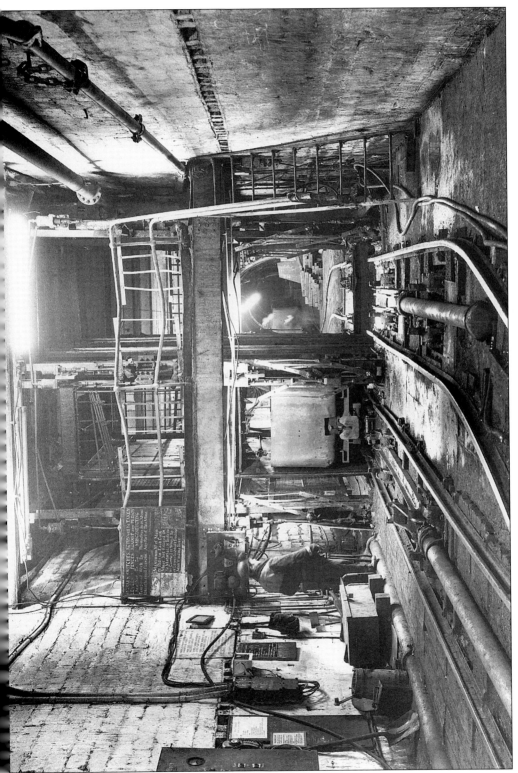

The shaft bottom taken in 1977.

A well-maintained main trunk road in 1977.

Left: Dai Mardon, Deputy on the V4 5ft seam, the Red Horizon in 1977.

Below: Chain hauled coal cutter on the Red Horizon, 1977.

Left: The last tram of coal raised in the Rhondda Valley on the 30 June 1986 Present were Mike Richards, the then Chairman of the Mardy Lodge, Eric Price who was the Lodge Secretary, Ivor England and the late Len Jones the Lodge treasurer.

Below: General view of colliery with the washery and pit head, 1980.

MARINE COLLIERY
EBBW VALE, MONMOUTH

The Ebbw Vale Steel, Iron and Coal Company Limited commenced the sinking of the Marine shafts in 1887; the shafts were completed in 1893. The downcast shaft was 18ft in diameter, and 1,254ft in depth. The upcast shaft was also 18ft in diameter and 1,242ft in depth, which included the sump. The two wrought iron headframes were constructed by Goddard, Massey & Warner of Nottingham.

The original winding engines were made by Nasmyth, Wilson and Co. of Patricroft, in 1890. The engine on the upcast shaft had two horizontal cylinders 41in. in diameter, a 6ft stroke, and a drum of 18ft diameter. The engine on the downcast shaft had 36in. cylinders, 6ft stroke, and a drum of 16ft. The engine on the upcast could raise 1,500 tons per day from the Old Coal seam.

The pumping engine, made by Hathorn Davey & Co. of Leeds, was placed under the winding engine on the downcast shaft. The engine and pumps could deal with 50,000 gallons of water per hour, when working at seven strokes per minute. Originally, ventilation was by a Schiele fan installed in 1891, driven by a compound steam engine; the fan had a diameter of 21ft, and could produce 120,000 cubic ft of air per minute. On 1 March 1927 the colliery suffered a disastrous explosion, when a firedamp ignition propagated by coal dust killed 52 men. In 1935 the Ebbw Vale Company sold all their collieries to Partridge, Jones & John Paton, Ltd., who then worked the colliery until Nationalisation in 1947.

In August 1982, a £2.5 million coal-winding improvement scheme was commissioned. The new high-speed pushbutton system of skip winding could raise over 500,000 tonnes of saleable coal in a year. In addition to the work in the shaft, a new coal handling plant was installed on the surface. The mine closed on 10 March 1989.

Above: The unusual cast iron structure was made at the Risca Foundry Newport, and appears to have been made from rising mains. This interesting structure was replaced around 1980.

Opposite page: A western class locomotive the *Western Consort* passing Marine Colliery in 1974.

Rising mains and pump rods from the Hathorn Davey pump in 1980.

Left: The removal of the Hathorn Davey engine's pump rod from the shaft. The rising mains were still in position in the brick lined shaft in the 1970s.

Below: The original main pumping engine at Marine Colliery, built by Hathorn Davey of Leeds in 1893. The engine has a 36in. high pressure cylinder and a 68in. low pressure cylinder with a 10ft stoke. This engine cost £4,630 to install.

Chainless haulage on the OC4s face on 15 October 1983.

Markham Colliery was situated in the Sirhowy Valley about 4 miles to the south of Tredegar. The sinking of the two shafts commenced in 1910 and was completed in 1913 by the Markham Steam Coal Co. Ltd. Both shafts the North (Upcast) and South (Downcast) shaft were 18ft in diameter and were sunk to the Old Coal seam at a depth of 1,800ft. The head frames were of lattice steel and 65ft high; the cages were originally single deck with two trams on the deck. The colliery was entirely electrically-powered, one of the earliest pits to be worked entirely by this means. The motors on the winding engines were made by Siemens Schuckert and the mechanical portion was by Markham & Co. of Chesterfield. The winding drums were semi-conical 12ft to 18ft in diameter. The colliery was ventilated by 2 Waddle fans of 18ft diameter each producing 400,000 cubic ft of air per minute.

The first face lighting to be installed on a face in the South Wales Coalfield in 1977.
Seventy face lighting units were installed on the M22 face, but damage occurred from falling stones and 40 units had to be returned to the manufacture for repair.
When working the system was very impressive, and was a credit to the face-team.

By the end of World War II all coal was worked on the long-wall system. The seams worked in 1946 were the Old Coal of which 50% was machine cut. The Big Vein was worked extensively throughout the take. The Yard Vein was worked by machine cutting and conveying. The upper Rhas Las seam was also worked by a conveyor system and had been worked thus since 1920. Pneumatic picks were used on the seam. Trunk conveyors were installed in April 1946. By the 1950s coal was wound in both shafts which were capable of raising 15,000 tons per week. At Vesting Day (1947) the workforce was 1,107 men underground, with 196 men working on the surface.

Like all pits in South Wales, Markham was brought up to date with modern mining technology, and in the 1960s and 1970s the production of high grade coking coal was around 230,000 tons per year.

By the late 1970s the colliery had around 10 miles of underground roadway with just over 3 miles of high-speed belt conveyors. By 1980 a major development linked Markham and the adjacent North Celynen to Oakdale, and Markham coal was taken directly underground to Oakdale for washing and grading. This three-pit complex was then the biggest single production unit in the South Wales Coalfield.

In December 1982 the men at Markham produced 8,641 tonnes of saleable coal in one week after a period of working in poor geological conditions. The 682ft long face was one and a half miles from pit bottom, and advanced 38ft in one week. At this period the colliery employed 615 men working on two faces. It closed in September 1985.

Markham Colliery before the rail connection was removed in 1974.

Markham Colliery yard in 1977.

The chain hauled shearer on the M22 face.

Merthyr Vale Colliery was the last venture of John Nixon, who commenced sinking with his partners on 23 August 1869, and proved the Four Feet seam on 1 January 1875. The first two trams of coal were raised on 4 December of the same year, and on the same day the first load of coal was forwarded to the market.

According to Charles Wilkins writing in 1888, "The colliery was known as the premier colliery in South Wales, and second only in depth, and magnitude of scientific appliances to Treharris".

A description of the pit in 1891 stated that two shafts were sunk about 255ft apart, the downcast and winding shaft was 16ft in diameter. The upcast also a winding shaft of 15ft in diameter, and was closed at the top by two wrought iron hoods, arranged so as to be lifted by the cage on its ascent. The shafts were tubbed or walled throughout.

I have been told on a number of occasions at pits in South Wales and other areas, that the winding engine had come from a ship or was a marine engine which was acquired by the colliery. But at Merthyr Vale Colliery the engine on the downcast shaft was really one of the very few engines which had been built as a marine engine for a large steamship.

The engine had been built by Maudslay, Son & Field of London; it had two 83in. horizontal cylinders with a 4ft stroke, two piston rods worked through the cylinder top to a crosshead, working directly to the shaft of a spiro-cylindrical drum which was 12ft in diameter at the first lift, and 24ft at the terminal lift. This drum was 16ft wide at the middle and weighed 60 tons. Even at the low pressure of 30 p.s.i. this was probably the most powerful engine for winding in the country in the 1890s. The winding engine on the upcast shaft had two 50in.

Merthyr Vale Colliery around 1900. As at Nixon's Navigation at Mountain Ash, the headframes had no backstays and were stabilised by chains or steel cables.

horizontal cylinders, 6ft stroke, direct-acting to a spiro-cylindrical drum. The cage on the downcast shaft carried two trams on one deck and was raised in 38 seconds, each train carried on an average 30 cwt. The colliery in 1891 was ventilated by a Waddle fan 40 ft in diameter which produced 230, 000 cubic ft of air per minute.

The permanent ventilator was on John Nixon's principle as at Deep Duffryn Colliery. The steam cylinder 48 in. diameter and 6 ft stroke, worked direct to the crankshaft, which carried two flywheels of 45 tons each. There were three air chambers 52ft high, 20ft wide and air pistons working in each, nearly touching the sides. The crank for the centre piston gave 6 ft stroke, and the cranks for the side pistons gave 7ft stroke. At nine revolutions there was calculated to be a circulation of 374,000 cubic ft of air per minute. There were also 528 inlet valves and 654 outlet valves, in three chambers, the valves having each 24in. by 22in.

As at Deep Duffryn Colliery the head-frames were constructed of old rails, and they still retained the wrought iron shackles for attaching the chains into the 1970s.

openings. By 1891 no accident or loss of life from explosion of gas had occurred, and no accident had occurred from overwinding at any of the Nixon Collieries.

For many years the colliery was owned by Nixons Navigation Steam Coal Company, but the concern was later to be known as Llewellyn (Nixon) Limited. In the 1930s the collieries were acquired by the Powell Duffryn Group who worked the colliery until nationalisation.

In the early 1960s a £2 million reorganisation scheme electrified the winding and increased the underground conveyor capacity. With a new coal preparation plant and rail wagon loading facilities on the surface, the pit became one of the major production units in South Wales. The workings in the 1970s and early 1980s were in an area 4 miles square and were in the Seven Feet seam. In 1974 the colliery made history with a record 45 cwts per manshift for every man on the colliery books. By the late 1970s the pit was turning an annual quarter of a million tons of high quality coal per year.

It is the aim of this book to highlight interesting features and the histories of some of the South Wales collieries, but I cannot overlook the appalling tragedy of the Aberfan Disaster of 1966 with the terrible loss of life of young children and adults. I feel that it must never be forgotten, and should the reader wish to know more I would recommend reading the Report into the Disaster at Aberfan of 1966, published by the HM Stationery Office, 1967.

The downcast shaft which was used as the coaling shaft.

The upcast shaft in 1977. By the 1970s the only original features were the headframes and heapstead.

Above: A typical roadway in Merthyr Vale Colliery. Note the device for arresting run away trams plus steel rings and road surfaces well covered in stone dust. Taken in 1981.

Left: A junction in the new B 50 development taken in 1981, again well covered in stone dust. This development was estimated to work an additional 3 millions of coal in the Seven Feet seam.

Above: A twin cylinder rope-changing capstan made by Uskside
Engineering, Newport, in 1881.

Opposite page top: A new development again in 1981.

Opposite page bottom: Timbering was still been undertaken in some areas of Merthyr Vale
Colliery in 1981.

Above: The morning shift arriving at the surface.

Opposite page: The afternoon shift waiting to descend.

In 1910 Thomas Taylor commenced the sinking of the two shafts at Nantgarw just to the north of the site of the famed Nantgarw Pottery which had ceased to work in 1822. The two shafts were extremely deep and were completed in 1915 to the depth of 2,568ft which was unprecedented for South Wales at that time.

The owners were the Taylor's Navigation Steam Coal Company Ltd., but by 1924 had sold out to the Taff Rhondda Navigation Steam Coal Company. This company ceased working in 1927 due to poor geological conditions and the colliery was sold to Powell Duffryn in 1927, who mothballed it.

In 1946 Powell Duffryn produced a scheme to work Nantgarw, which had been drawn up in 1937 but delayed by World War II. The plan was to work the mine on the horizon mining method, but the advent of Nationalisation permitted areas of coal to be worked from the Nantgarw shafts which were not previously part of the Nantgarw take. The colliery was reconstructed under the NCB and worked successfully until 1974, when the NCB decided to link Nantgarw and Windsor Pits into a single unit, working the Windsor seams but winding the coal at Nantgarw to the modern washery.

In 1977 losses were over of £1 million but by May 1978 the loss was transformed to a profit of over £40,000 per month, for a chainless haulage system, and Anderson Strathclyde ranging drum shear had raised output to over 5,000 tonnes per week. At this time the F44 coalface produced a record 334 cwts per manshift, which were amongst the best in South Wales and the best ever recorded by Nantgarw/Windsor.

An 1978 NCB press release stated that "Nantgarw/Windsor is one of the coalfield's premier collieries, linked by a £1.75 million project. The colliery will exploit over 9 million tonnes of coking coal, which will keep the mine in business well into the next century."

In 1985 Nantgarw incurred losses of £5 million, and in 1986 a further £4 million was lost in 6 months. British Coal said that output results from two districts affected by worsening and uncertain geological conditions had continued to decline. The area director said that he could see no justification for continuing mining operations at Nantgarw, because of the collieries' uncertain geology.

Nantgarw/Windsor closed in 1986.

Left: Cold wet conditions at the bottom of the Nantgarw Downcast shaft.

Opposite page: Nantgarw Colliery in 1978.

Aerial view of the Nantgarw coking plant, 1978.

A cable hauled manriding train at the bottom of the Nantgarw incline.

A junction in the new development at Nantgarw in 1977. A high speed cable belt is on the right of the picture.

An abandoned concrete lined roadway taken in 1977.

Above:
Reconditioned Gullick Dobson chocks waiting to be taken inbye in 1977.

Left: An Anderson Strathclyde ranging drum shear on a chainless haulage face F44s, in 1978.

Although never worked by the NCB, the colliery was situated in the curtilage of Deep Duffryn Colliery, which used the two shafts as a pumping station and for the ventilation. Work began on the colliery in 1855, but it was only five years later that it produced coal. When sunk it was said to be the deepest colliery in Wales and eventually closed in 1941.

The South Pit was originally sunk 1095ft to the Four Feet seam and 1,275ft to the Nine ,Feet seam. A later depth was given by the NCB as 1,353ft to the Graig seam. The shaft was divided into two, with one half serving the Four Feet seam and the other half winding from the Nine Feet seam, with a total diameter of 18ft. In the 1890s this shaft worked with two winding engines, which had two 33in. oscillating cylinders, with a 6ft stroke, both engines had spiral drums, ranging from 10ft diameter at the first lift and 20ft at the termination.

On the North Pit stood the last large Waddle fan in the South Wales coalfield which was 42ft in diameter and was driven by a double-ended steam engine also made by Waddles of Llanelli. This magnificent monument to Victorian engineering was broken up in the early 1980s despite its supposed protection as a listed monument.

The South Pit was latterly used as a pumping station by the NCB which also took water from the abandoned Abergorki Colliery situated just to the south, which worked from 1922 until closure in 1967.

General view of Nixon's Navigation Colliery around 1910, the massive headframes had no backstays but were stabilised by steel cables. The last Waddle fan can be seen on the extreme right hand edge of the picture.

The Waddle Fan just before demolition. The fan engine was taken to Big Pit Mining Museum and the fan was broken up.

The engine house for the Waddle fan, the fan itself and northern end of the heapstead, taken in 1975. Note the expansion band in the piping.

Above: The headframe and engine house of the Navigation's South pit in 1977.

Above: The abandoned pit bottom of the North Pit on which the Waddle fan was situated, in 1977.

The double ended engine for the Waddle fan now situated at Big Pit, Blaenavon. Should one cylinder fail the connecting rod was reconnected to the second cylinder to ensure that there was a continuous power source to the fan.

Sir John an Avonside locomotive built in Bristol in 1914 as Avonside No.1680, and was disused by 1972. This photograph was taken when it was still working.

Above: The Mountain Ash shed around 1977 The disused engine is the *Earl*, a Peckett No. 1203 of 1910. The engine on the right is *Sir Gomer*, a Peckett No.1859 built in 1932.

Above: A Hudswell Clarke engine working a coal train up to the Phurnacite plant at Abercwmboi around 1979.

Sir Gomer in 1979 with the Navigation headframe in the background.

The colliery was sunk by the Oakdale Navigation Collieries Ltd., a subsidiary of the Tredegar Iron & Coal Company Ltd. Sinking commenced in 1907 and was completed to the steam coal measures in 1911.

There were three shafts originally sunk to the following depths:

The South Pit, the downcast 21ft in diameter, originally sunk to the Upper Rhas Las seam at depth of 2,040ft. This was the coal winding shaft.

The North Pit the upcast shaft 21ft in diameter, sunk to the Old Coal seam which was found at a depth of 2,202ft.

A third shaft was the Waterloo Pit also a downcast 17ft 6in. in diameter and sunk to the Red Ash seam at a depth of 286ft.

The headframe of the South Pit was built by Rees & Kirby at a height of 76ft to the centre of the pulleys which were 20ft in diameter. The steam winding engine on the South Pit was built by Markham & Co. of Chesterfield with 36in. cylinders and a 7ft stroke. A semi-conical drum with a diameter of 27ft was installed in 1945. The cages on the South Pit were, in 1945, double deck each carrying two trams, each tram carrying 25 cwt of coal. The average weight of coal raised per wind was about 5 tons.

The North Pit head frame was originally 83ft high with a steam winding engine by Messrs Markham & Co.. It too had 36in. diameter cylinders with a 7ft stroke, although the drum was 28ft in diameter.

The headframe on the Waterloo shaft was only 55ft high with single deck cages for two trams each. The engine house on the North Pit was built of ferro-concrete, and the pit boxing was similarly constructed. The colliery had twelve Babcock & Wilcox double drum water tube boilers, with a working pressure of 200 psi. A power-house with a large water cooling tower dominated the colliery surface. Two Sirocco fans each 154in. in diameter produced 600,000 cubic ft of air per minute.

The output of coal in the first 50 years had been obtained from the Meadow, Rhas Las and Big veins. The Meadow Vein varied from 6ft to 7ft in thickness and was worked on the longwall system, conveyor filled, and machine cut. The Rhas Las seam was 6ft 6in. thick, and was also worked on a longwall system.

The Red Ash seam, 2ft 10in. thick, was only worked at the Waterloo Pit or House Coal shaft.

The Oakdale Colliery Village was also built in 1908-10 by the Oakdale Navigation Collieries Ltd. It was designed by A.F. Webb, the company architect. When built, it was considered to be a model village: it was probably one of the first mining villages to be built in South Wales to have grass margins between the road and pavements, and many houses had front gardens, a unique feature in South Wales at the time. A three or four bedroom house cost £350 to build, and was let at a rent of 9s a week, inclusive of rates and taxes which were about 2s 6d. A smaller house was let for 5s a week. Even the smaller houses were provided with a bathroom.

After the General Strike came the first shaker conveyor, which was the start of mechanisation at Oakdale. By 1929-1930 the yearly output of the Steam Coal Colliery was one million tons. In the 1930s coal cutting machines and a conveyor were installed in the Big Vein and brought the production of coal back to reasonable output again, so that some of the unemployed men were taken on again before the outbreak of World War II. A second outburst of water occurred in the Old Coal vein which was just being developed. A second exit was driven into the seam in twelve weeks, and the problem was eventually overcome.

After Vesting Day in 1947 the shaker conveyors were replaced by modern belt conveyors, the stall and heading system ceased and miners worked next to each other on the coal face. The 18in. and 20in. conveyors were finally replaced by the 40in. wide conveyor. The workforce at Vesting Day for the three pits was 1,911 men working underground, with 343 men on the surface. Four seams were worked in the late 1940s, the Big Vein, Meadow Vein, Upper Rhas Las and the Waterloo Red Ash in the Waterloo Pit. In the 1950s the average weight of coal raised on the South Pit by the steam winding engine was about 5 tons, the maximum winding capacity of the engine was 50 winds per hour.

In 1959 for the third time water burst into the workings in the Old Coal and the colliery flooded, the electricity supply to the pumps was lost and it was only the diversion of the water into a heading, while the pumps were not working, which saved the colliery.

In 1980 a major reorganisation linked Markham and North Celynen pits at a cost of £12.5 million. By the 1980s fourteen miles of high-speed, computer-controlled conveyors carried coal from seven faces at the three collieries to the Oakdale shaft, where skips wound coal at a rate of 420 tonnes per hour. To prolong the life of the pit a further development was undertaken and new roadways were driven into an area of reserves thought to be around 9.8 million tonnes, south of Oakdale and near to the closed Wyllie Colliery. From 1975 to 1985 the NCB had invested £23 million in the Oakdale Complex.

An NCB press release stated that the reserves for Oakdale Colliery were estimated at more than 22 million tonnes, and the pit was numbered amongst the coalfield's long-life producers, with a combined annual output target of 900,000 tonnes. In the last week in April 1986 the colliery produced a record 21,071 tonnes of coking coal, its highest output since April 1979, putting the colliery on course to return to profits after the previous year's loss of £7.2 million. In November of that year the colliery produced 25,300 tonnes of coal.

The colliery was closed by British Coal in 1989.

Conveyor attendant.

The colliery around 1910 with sinking still in process.

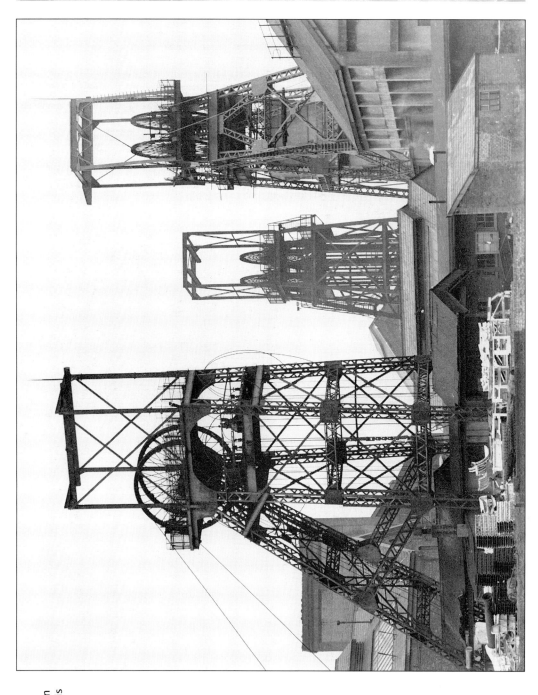

The three pit heads in 1974; the headframe in the foreground is the Waterloo or house coal pit.

A development
heading.

Roadway with a high speed conveyor at the demarcation line between Oakdale and North Celynen.

Oakdale pit bottom, 1978.

Electric Locomotive near the pit bottom.

A repair gang at work.

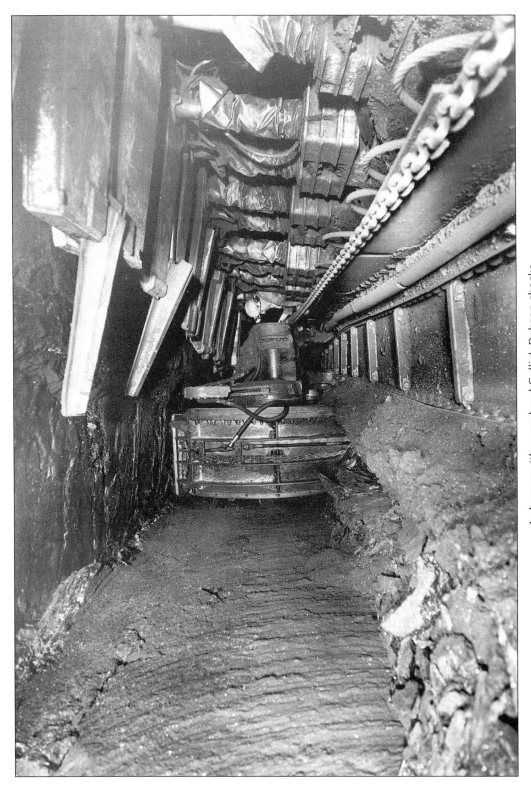

A shearer with a cowl and Gullick Dobson chocks.

Transfer point near the pit bottom.

A typical Powell Duffryn pit which, although impressive with its vast central engine house for winding engines, compressors and generators, not particularly attractive when compared to Deep Navigation or Deep Duffryn Collieries.

Sinking began in 1906 and the shafts were completed by 1909; the two shafts were 2,400 and 1,955ft in depth with a diameter of 21ft. The manpower rose to a 3,208 by the early 1930's, and the colliery output was around 860,000 tons per year. The colliery was one of the first pits in South Wales to install the Meco-Moore coal cutter. It was electrified in 1962-63 and £2$^1/_2$ million were spent on a modernisation project, which included the deepening of the mine to new working levels at a depth of 2,400ft. By the 1970's the Penallta take was around four square miles, bounded on the west by the Gelligaer Fault on the west and the massive Penydarren fault on the east.

In 1979-80 all coaling was in the Seven Feet seam and eight miles of underground roadways and two and a half miles of high speed conveyor belt were at work.

£3$^1/_2$ million were allocated to Penallta Colliery in the end of 1985 for a heavy-duty high-technology coal face, the same year plans were made to install rapid coal winding skips which were hoped would raise shaft capacity by 33 per cent.

Despite of the new equipment and investment the colliery ceased workings in 1991

The Colliery Lamp room with Garforth Safety lamps in the foreground and Thomas & Williams' workman's lamps in the rear.

The downcast and coaling pit in the foreground and upcast shaft in the background. In the 1980s there was major modernisation here.

General view of Penallta colliery from the baths, with the afternoon shift waiting to descend.

The compressors and electric winder for the downcast shaft in the distance at Penallta.

Low face at the colliery with chain haulage and chocks.

The sinking of this colliery was begun in 1872 by John and David Glasbrook and a Mr Yeo of Swansea. One year later they were joined by Messrs Cory Brothers. The man in charge of the sinking was David Thomas (Cwmbach). The sinking was very hazardous, as running sand and inrushes of water were encountered. To overcome these problems a large beam-type pump was installed in a chamber in the No. 2 shaft. Sinking continued until the Nine Feet seam was won in 1878 at a depth of 1,752ft. For some years coal was wound for internal use on a small single sheave pitch-pine headframe, the later steel headgear being constructed around the original headframe about 1901. By 1901 the building of the No. 2 (southern) engine house was completed and a steam winding engine by Thornewell & Wareham was installed and ran until replaced by an electric winder in 1957. The date on the engine house of the No. 1 shaft was 1905 and we can assume that this was the date of the completion of this shaft and engine house. The original steam winder was kept working whilst a second engine house for the new electric winder was constructed on the opposite side of the upcast shaft. Apart from the box-like structures for the new electric winding houses, many of the main buildings remained as built until 1985, when the colliery was closed and levelled.

The smaller house coal shaft was sunk around 1912 and was fitted with a Robey steam winding engine. Winding on the house coal shaft is said to have ceased around 1949.

By the middle of World War II the six or seven highly productive seams were exhausted within the original colliery take, but working was extended to an adjacent area of unworked coal from Cwmcynon Colliery, which was also acquired by Powell Duffryn. After Nationalisation the colliery take was two and a quarter miles square.

In the 1960s and early 1970s the weekly average saleable output was 4000 tons. A major reorganisation in the early 1960s streamlined loading and conveying and 800 men produced an annual 180,000 tons, for the Phurnacite plant and domestic market. The then mining programme worked an area of four miles square, with more than ten miles of underground roadways and over three miles of high speed belt conveyors.

The colliery was closed by British Coal in 1985.

The lamproom in 1980.

The headframe on the upcast shaft had been turned round when the steam winder was decommissioned and the new electric winder built to the east of the shaft.

A Robey Steam winder on the house coal shaft. It was dismantled in the late 1970s.

A development heading.

Conveyor belt suspended from steel rings.

The pit bottom in 1978.

Above: Chain-hauled shearer on the coal face 1977.

Left: Cast iron beam of a Cornish pumping engine made by Harvey of Hayle in 1858, situated in a large chamber half way down the No.2 shaft. The beam was used as a counterweight on the pumping engine rods.

Left: Flat rope for Uskside winding engine.

Below: Compressed air, twin-cylinder Uskside haulage engine, which was located on an underground stable pit, near the pit bottom.

SIX BELLS COLLIERY
(ARRAEL GRIFFIN 4 AND 5)
SIX BELLS, MONMOUTH

John Lancaster & Co. commenced the sinking of Arrael Griffin in 1891; coal winding commenced several years later. There was a period of seven years from 1930 when the colliery was stopped due to lack of trade. In 1936 the colliery was taken over by Partridge, Jones & John Paton Ltd. who then worked it until Nationalisation. Vivian Colliery closed in 1958 and for several years the Vivian shaft became a downcast for Six Bells.

The early 1960s saw the electrification of the winding engines; in the early 1970s, the colliery was linked underground to Marine which then wound all the coal from Six Bells. In 1983 the only seam being worked was the Garw.

On 28 June 1960 an ignition of firedamp occurred at about 10.45 a.m. near the 0.10 face in the W district of the Old Coal seam. The coal dust was ignited and the explosion spread through the district, killing 45 of the 48 men working there at the time. The public enquiry, which was held later, felt that the firedamp could have been ignited by an incendiary spark caused by a fall of quartzitic stone on to a steel canopy.

Seams worked at Six Bells
Elled
Big Vein
Threequarter
Black Vein
Meadow Vein
Old Coal; Garw.

A Torque Tension track-mounted hydraulic drilling rig. This drill advanced a tunnel in the Garw rock by 51ft a week, more than double the previous best. The machine would drill a 7ft hole in hard rock in one minute and 20 seconds, compared with 30 minutes using a hand held drill.

Above: Six Bells in 1979.

Opposite page: The tub circuit in 1976.

Above: Full tubs near the pit bottom. Soon after this was taken, all coal was carried underground to Marine Colliery.

Left: Hand packed gob plough face in the Garw seam.

Opposite page: Overman on chock face in the Garw seam, 1978.

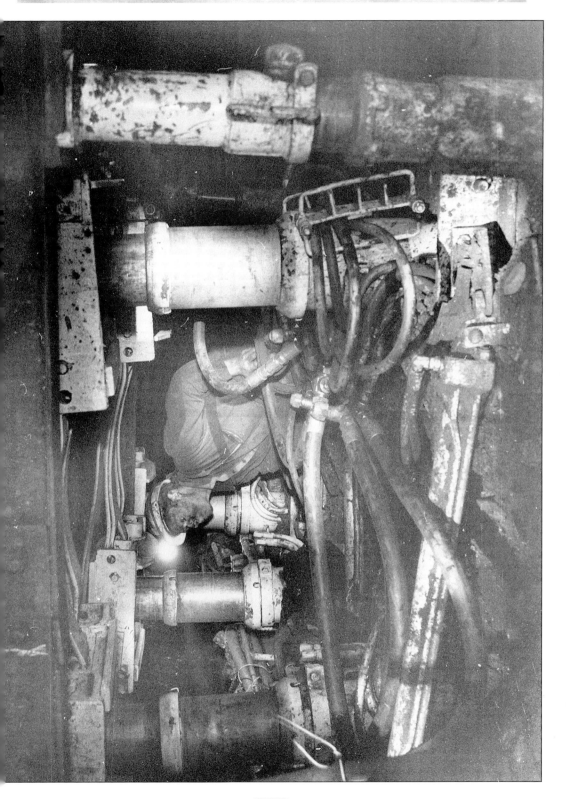

TIRPENTWYS COLLIERY
PONTYPOOL, MONMOUTH

The sinking of the two shafts at Tirpentwys Colliery commenced around 1878 and the first coal was raised in 1881 as the colliery first appears in the Inspectors' List of Mines for that year. The first owners were Darby & Norris, but by 1884 Tirpentwys was owned by the Tirpentwys Colliery Co. Several years later the Tirpentwys Black Vein Steam Coal & Coke Co. was formed and this concern continued to operate the colliery until Nationalisation in 1947.

The downcast shaft was 16ft in diameter, depth 1,326ft. The upcast shaft was 14ft in diameter, depth 1,278ft.

The original colliery winding engine was of the vertical type and was made by Daglish & Co. with two vertical cylinders 40 in. in diameter, and a stroke of 6 ft.

Seams worked at Tirpentwys Colliery: The Elled, Big Vein, Three Quarter Seam, Black Vein Seam, Meadow Vein and Old Coal seam.

The colliery ceased coaling in 1969, but the shafts and winders were retained for pumping and ventilation and, since coal from Blaenserchan Colliery was routed underground to Hafodyrynys Colliery via Tirpentwys, for washing and dispatch on British Rail.

Right: Tirpentwys in 1975. The colliery closed in 1969, but was retained for pumping and ventilation. The fine vertical engine housed an electric winder by Wild & Co; the unusual headframe was designed to work with a large vertical steam winding engine.

Opposite page: Engine house and fan of a Walker fan.

Right: A set of early electric three-throw pumps on the Tillery Landing.

Opposite page: The pit bottom of the down cast shaft.

TOWER COLLIERY
HIRWAUN, GLAMORGAN

Together with Betws Mine, Tower Colliery is the last large mine operating in the South Wales Coalfield.

A very large number of mines, drifts and shafts have been worked on the northern flank of the Rhigos Mountain over a period of two hundred years. The present drift mine was driven in 1920, and the new No. 3 was driven in 1958-59 and was the fourth drift to have been driven under the name Tower. The shaft known as Tower No. 4 was sunk from 1941-44. A drift mine known as Tirherbert Colliery was situated about 3,000ft to the west of Tower Drift, this mine was driven in 1914 and closed in December 1958. The mine was owned by Llewellyn & Sons, a subsidiary of Powell Duffryn, and employed 320 men underground in 1937; 194 men worked at the mine when it closed in 1958.

Tower and Fernhill Collieries were linked in 1964 to form a single unit of 860 men who produced 250,000 tons of semi-anthracite which was brought to the surface at Tower drift. Much of this production was used at the Phurnacite plant.

By the late 1970s the colliery take covered an area of around four square miles and the Five Feet and Nine Feet seams were worked. The take was heavily faulted which displaced the coal up to 164ft vertically in places. The colliery operated ten miles of underground roadway with more than seven miles of high-speed conveyors.

Tower Colliery was also the last mine in South Wales to use pit ponies which appear to have been made redundant when the last miners' strike began. The mine was estimated to have workable reserves of 3.6 million tonnes in 1980. By 1985 production improved and a press release stated that the pit must achieve an output of 6,000 saleable tonnes of coal per week to become financially solvent. A press release of June 1986 announced investment of £5 million in a new generation of double telescopic power roof supports in the V29 coal face in the Five/Seven Feet seam, where anthracite was up to 10ft thick. This face would have a powerful 500hp power loading machine with two cutting drums which profiled the roadways at each end of the face. It was hoped that the face would have an output of at least 1,200 tonnes per day, and probably more. It was also in this year that the coal was brought through the mountain from Mardy Colliery to Tower.

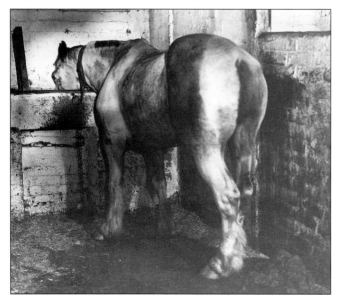

Tower Colliery was eventually sold to an employee buy-out team in 1984, who set back to work 239 men each contributing £8,000 to the £2 million buy-out fund, and the pit is still at work in 2001.

Left: Rex in his stall at Tower Colliery in 1979.

Opposite page: Rex at work in Tower Colliery in 1979.

Above: Rex with his ostler in 1979.

Opposite page: Typical conditions at Tower, a high speed conveyor and attendants.

The afternoon shift waiting to descend at an air lock in 1980.

More of the afternoon shift waiting outside the lamproom in 1980.

The early history of the old Tymawr shaft is obscure. In 1891 the *Colliery Guardian* reported "This shaft was sunk many years ago to the depth of 600ft, and is oval in form 16ft by 10ft. It has recently been sunk from 600ft to the 5ft seam, a depth of some 1,500ft".

In the 1890s the Great Western Company continued to expand. In the year 1891 its mineral property was around 2,200 acres, but by 1898 it was over 3,000 acres, and 3,500 men were producing almost 1,000,000 tons of coal annually. Maritime Colliery was acquired by the Great Western Company in 1893; Cwm Colliery was the last major development of the Great Western Company, its sinking being commenced at Beddau in 1909.

At the turn of the century all coal was being worked on the longwall method, with stalls 36 or 42ft wide, and cross roads every 150ft. To increase the safety of the workings, an elaborate system of sprays and hosepipes was installed in the roads to water the dust. Explosives were not used in the steam coal seams.

Despite the elaborate safety precautions, an explosion of firedamp killed 58 men in August 1892, though the cause of ignition was not known. On 11 April 1893 a fire broke out underground, killing 63 men; it was caused by sparks from the brake of a hauling engine igniting flammable material.

In 1923 the No. 2 and No. 3 shafts, and the old Tymawr shaft, were abandoned. The New Tymawr shaft (known as No. 1) was sunk, and the Hetty shaft was retained for pumping and ventilation. Today only the headframe and winding engine house and steam winding engine of the Hetty Pit survive. The original intention was to incorporate the Hetty Pit into the Rhondda Heritage Museum, but this intention seems to have lapsed and the future of this interesting relic is now not clear.

The Tymawr Colliery site is now mainly covered by housing.

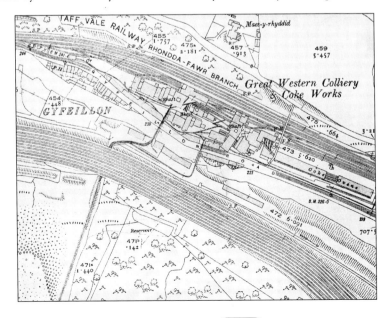

The Great Western Colliery around 1900.

Above: The Great Western Colliery c.1910, from left to right.
The Hetty Pit, No. 3 shaft and the No. 2 shaft.

Above: A coal train from Mardy Colliery passing the engine house of the Hetty Pit.

General view of Tymawr Colliery in 1983 with the screens and washery to the left; the offices and winder are on the right.

Tymawr Colliery around 1900. A general view with the air compressor house in the foreground, the boilers and pit-head of the old Tymawr Colliery. The colliery was closed in 1923.

Right: The Barker & Cope winding engine built at Kidsgrove, Staffordshire in 1875.
Originally built with two 40in. cylinders and Cornish valves, later fitted with new 36in. cylinders and piston valves. The drum is 16ft in diameter and originally held flat rope. This engine had been run on compressed air for many years.
After years of being neglected and vandalised, the engine is now undergoing restoration by a group of local enthusiasts and has recently been turned over on compressed air.

Opposite page: The late George Downs, the last winding engine man on the Hetty Pit, in 1983.

Above: A abandoned roadway in the No. 2 Rhondda seam; note the sandstone roof with no means of support.

Left: A vertical twin cylinder pump with banjo connecting rods, situated in the No. 2 landing of the Hetty Shaft.

Dick, one of the Tymawr shaftsmen, carrying out the routine inspection of the Hetty shaft from the roof of the cage, in 1983.

Looking back up the Hetty shaft, with movement showing in the shaft walling.
The shaft was sunk by the Great Western Colliery Company in 1875 to the Six Feet seam at a
depth of 1,176ft.

Above: Bill Pember and Dick the shaftsmen at Tymawr and the Hetty Pit, inspecting an early horizontal steam pump with banjo framed connecting rods. The engine was said to have been made by the Colliery engineer and blacksmith.
The engine is situated in a lodge in the No. 3 shaft, and was reached by riding on the roof of the cage and proceeding through the original workings.

Left: 612 Face using props and bars in 1978.

The last dram of coal raised at Tymawr Colliery in June 1983.

Bill Pember and the remains of the last ventilation furnace to survive in South Wales. This furnace was situated on the No. 3 landing in the Hetty shaft, and was originally located under the arch of firebricks which prevented the furnace from overheating the strata above. This furnace dates from the late 1870s.

WYNDHAM AND
WESTERN COLLIERIES
NANT-Y-MOEL, GLAMORGAN

Wyndham Colliery was sunk in 1865 by James Brogden who soon went into liquidation when the Colliery was bought by Colonel North and became part of North's Navigation Company. The colliery was sold to Cory Brothers in 1906, but by 1942 it was sold to Powell Duffryn who continued to work the pit until Nationalisation.

Western Colliery was sunk in 1872-76 by David Davies of the Ocean Coal Company who worked the Two Feet Nine seam, Lower Six Feet seam, the Upper and Lower Nine Feet seams, and by the 1970s workings were concentrated in the Bute, Five Feet and Gellideg seams.

Both collieries were linked in 1965 after deepening the shafts to 1,440ft, and 900 men worked an area of about 16 square miles. The colliery had over eight miles of underground roadway with five miles of high-speed conveyors. It closed in January 1984.

The shaft of Western Colliery recently used for men, materials and ventilation.

Wyndham from the air in 1978.

The Pit heads at Wyndham with the Western shaft in the distance.
Note the new or reconditioned chocks waiting to be taken underground.

Steam haulage engine built Llewellyn & Cubit, Pentre, Rhondda Valley, 1884.

Official and cylinder cover of the Llewellyn & Cubit haulage engine, 1979.

Deputy in old stables inspecting distressed timber.

Above: Turntable near pit bottom at Wyndham.

Above: The pit bottom at Wyndham shaft.

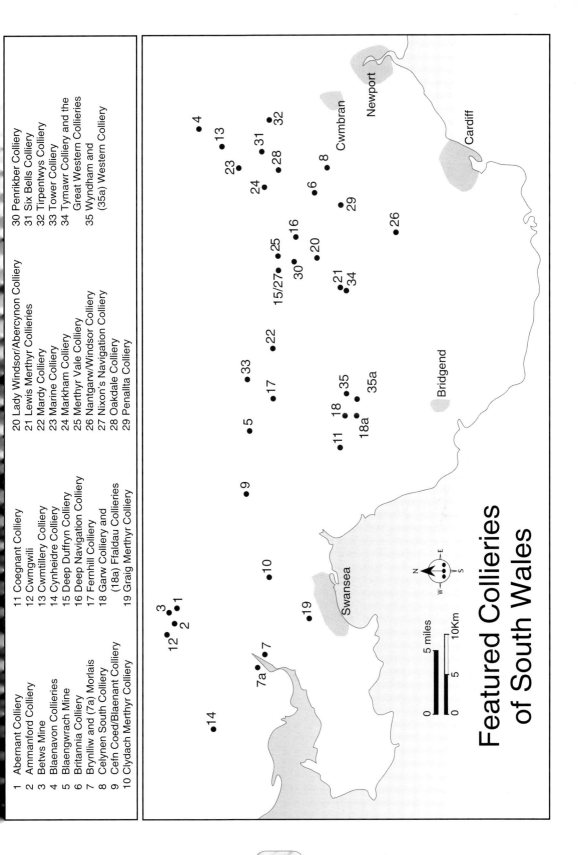

Featured Collieries of South Wales

1 Abernant Colliery
2 Ammanford Colliery
3 Betws Mine
4 Blaenavon Collieries
5 Blaengwrach Mine
6 Britannia Colliery
7 Brynlliw and (7a) Morlais
8 Celynen South Colliery
9 Cefn Coed/Blaenant Colliery
10 Clydach Merthyr Colliery
11 Coegnant Colliery
12 Cwmgwili
13 Cwmtillery Colliery
14 Cynheidre Colliery
15 Deep Duffryn Colliery
16 Deep Navigation Colliery
17 Fernhill Colliery
18 Garw Colliery and
    (18a) Ffaldau Collieries
19 Graig Merthyr Colliery
20 Lady Windsor/Abercynon Colliery
21 Lewis Merthyr Collieries
22 Mardy Colliery
23 Marine Colliery
24 Markham Colliery
25 Merthyr Vale Colliery
26 Nantgarw/Windsor Colliery
27 Nixon's Navigation Colliery
28 Oakdale Colliery
29 Penallta Colliery
30 Penrikber Colliery
31 Six Bells Colliery
32 Tirpentwys Colliery
33 Tower Colliery
34 Tymawr Colliery and the
    Great Western Collieries
35 Wyndham and
    (35a) Western Colliery

INDEX

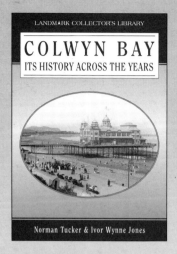
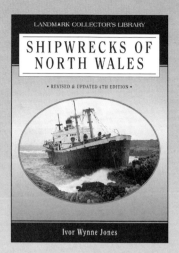
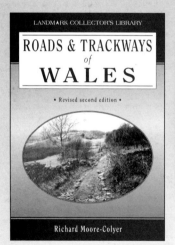

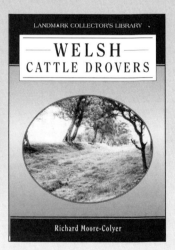